Daniel Kelley McBride

SO YOU WANT TO MOVE TO PORTUGAL...

Your Ultimate Guide to Retiring in Portugal

Daniel Kelley McBride
Almada, Setubal, Portugal
DanMcBride.PT@gmail.com

ISBN: 9798389979642

Requests: danmcbride.pt@gmail.com

DEDICATION

To my husband, Timm — for taking this 18 year ride with me, and for this grand journey to Portugal! Your support continues to be invaluable!

ACKNOWLEDGEMENTS

Timm McBride "I have to start by thanking my awesome husband, Timm. From reading early drafts to offering design expertise for the cover, and endless support, he has been as important to getting this book done as I was. Thank you so much."

Tracey Faulkinbury "whose editing skillfulness and keen eye has helped make this endeavor so much more than it otherwise could have been — thank you for all your help and support."

Jamie Matteson "for your consistent friendship, support, and impeccable proofreading skills — thank you for your expertise."

Russell Loring "whose encouragement, support, and editing helped make this project become a reality."

Portugal Expat Community "who continually share their knowledge and experiences with each other on social media, and in expat meet-up groups. Your shared knowledge encourages all of us to reach our dreams, whether to move to another country, learn the local language and customs, or to write a book about it."

ABOUT THE AUTHOR

Daniel Kelley McBride, MS

Dan McBride is a father, husband, singer, and dog lover; spending many years singing in men's choruses, and serving in non-profit organization management. Professionally, after earning Associate and Bachelor of Science degrees at Boise State University, and a Master of Science in Physician Assistant Studies at Pacific University, Dan practiced medicine as a PA in Washington, Oregon, and California. His most recent accomplishment was retiring and moving to Portugal with his husband Timm and dog Bubba. *So You Want to Move to Portugal* shares tips they learned in that process.

PROLOGUE

So you want to move to Portugal - I hear that a lot. It seems to be the "in" thing right now. It seems every time I turn around, someone is saying they are thinking about moving to Portugal. In spite of all the surrounding noise, once the idea of moving to Portugal got my attention, I've become hyperaware of everything I hear about Portugal. Nevertheless, I do hear a lot about people in the United States talking about moving to Portugal.

Our journey began a couple years ago when we ramped up our search for an appropriate place to spend our retirement years. That was before the COVID-19 pandemic.

Needless to say, enduring a worldwide pandemic changed lives in many ways: Our jobs and careers, home life, relationships, recreational patterns, and life goals. It became clear by the end of the second year of COVID that we had become ready to retire and pull the trigger on our retirement plans - in Portugal.

TABLE OF CONTENTS

CHAPTER 1

WHY PORTUGAL?

We get asked that a lot. Why Portugal? Why would you ever move out of the United States? Well, let's just say that Portugal has a lot to offer.

Overlooking the Alfama district of Lisbon with a view across the Tagus River - Timm McBride

Here are my Top 10 Reasons to live in Portugal

1. Weather

Tired of the cold and rain? As we all recognize, our mood can be significantly influenced by the weather. (think Seasonal Affective Disorder) The excellent weather, especially during spring and summer is why people in Portugal always seem to be in a good mood. We like the temperate climate of Portugal, which varies throughout the country. Nearer the coastlines, the weather is cooler. The North can get quite cool and very wet in winter. Larger cities can be warmer and drier, as can the Algarve down South and some of the more inland areas. Are you ready for more than 300 days of sunshine?

2. Geography

We love a variety of scenery. Landscapes that spark our enthusiasm include mountains, oceans, valleys, farmland and vineyards, rivers, lakes, and everything in between.

Fortunately, Portugal has all of these landscapes and more. Portugal is located on the western most point in Europe and convenient to most of the rest of Europe

Panoramic view of Almada overlooking the Tagus River - Timm McBride

and the UK. Thanks to its relatively small size, you can get to know the most important cities and sites quite easily.

Porto wins "Best City" award

The city of Porto has been voted the "Best City Destination in the World 2022" at the World Travel Awards ceremony.

The World Travel Awards, "considered the 'Oscars' of tourism," brought together major decision-makers and prominent figures in the sector (Source: TPN/Lusa).

Downtown Porto - Timm McBride

The very best beaches in the world have been revealed by TripAdvisor, with one beach from the Algarve making the top ten. Praia da Falesia, located in Olhos de Agua, Portugal, took the sixth spot in the list and was one of only two European beaches to make the cut.

Lagos beach, in the Algarve - Timm McBride

One TripAdvisor reviewer wrote of the beach: "Gorgeous red sand cliffs lead to the green-blue ocean and a white sand beach that seemingly stretches forever." (Source: *The Portugal News)*

3. Safe Environment

As we considered where to move abroad, a concern that became increasingly important was our personal safety. Not only do we have to consider the fact that we are a same-sex married couple, but we also began worrying about the increasing violence we saw happening around us in the United States.

The good news is that Portugal is often considered one of the safest countries in Europe to visit and live. It even ranked third out of 163 countries on the Global Peace Index.

The index is scored by considering factors like crime rate, terrorist acts, violent demonstrations, political scene, and relations with other countries.

Portugal is a peaceful country. We experience no anxiety about gun violence, carjackings, and violent crime in general. Drugs have been decriminalized here and are not an obvious problem. We feel safe everywhere we have gone, including walking in the city late at night. Most people here say they feel the same sense of personal security.

4. LGBTQ+ Equality

Portugal is LGBTQ+ friendly and has recognized same-sex unions since 2001 and same-sex marriage since 2010, when it was written into the country's constitution. The constitution also bans discrimination against LGBTQ+ people. Importantly, in reality, we have not experienced any discrimination and continue to feel safe.

LGBTQ+ Pride is evident in Portugal

The IGLTA website, the world's leading network of LGBTQ+ welcoming tourism businesses, worked with Destination Pride to develop a database that makes it easy to see how countries rank for LGBTQ+ travelers. Our adopted country resides at the top of the list. The 2019 Eurobarometer public opinion poll said that 74 percent of the Portuguese people supported same-sex marriage. Both of the largest cities, Lisbon and Porto, have good-sized LGBTQ+ communities.

Lisbon has a very popular and well attended Gay Pride Festival and parade and also hosts the international Queer Lisboa Gay and Lesbian Film Festival every year, too.

5. Quality Healthcare

According to InternationalLiving.com, Portugal has some of the best healthcare in the world, ranked number 12 by the World Health Organization, far above the U.S. which comes in at 37.

Serviço Nacional de Saúde (SNS)
Portugal's Public Health System

Doctors are less hurried and happy to take their time to discuss all of the health concerns of the patient treating them as individuals instead of just numbers.

Contributing to these high results are strong rankings in infrastructure, privacy, patient rights, accessibility, and relatively short waiting times. And there's no arguing with the outcome. Portuguese people enjoy an average life expectancy of 81 years. By comparison, the expected life span of someone born in the U.S. is now 76.4 years — the shortest it has been in nearly two decades.

6. Lifestyle

Another consideration for us was how well we would be able to establish a new life when moving abroad. Fortunately, Portugal has a well-earned reputation for being warm and welcoming. This friendly attitude is extended to visitors as well as foreigners like us who decide to stay in the country long-term.

Lisbon City Life

A typical workday ends around 6 PM and after that, it's all about relaxing. Having drinks in a pub or having a nice dinner are a few activities that can demonstrate how good life is in Portugal. *Forbes.com* has also listed Portugal as one of the best places for residency and possibly a second passport, through citizenship. Portugal is a country that offers the best of two worlds. It is a sanctuary where you can enjoy the cosmopolitan city life in the morning and find yourself laying down at a world-class beach in the afternoon. In 2021, Portugal was widely reported to be one of the healthiest and most clean-living places to live.

7. Affordability

Portugal's overall low living cost, high quality of life, and the exceptional value of property prices are also motivations for ex-pats to move here; and the community just keeps growing. If you are considering relocating to Portugal, the country offers a favorable tax jurisdiction for financially prudent, and high-net-worth investors.

Lisbon Street View - Timm McBride

While we would not want to mislead anyone that you can live for next to nothing in Portugal, the value and quality of life here is excellent. We can eat wonderfully well and enjoy wine and dessert for a reasonable price at local restaurants. Using public transportation is quite easy and very affordable. Also, there are so many places, activities, and experiences we can enjoy that cost us little or nothing that we have lots to keep us busy while also keeping to a reasonable budget.

For an example, from *Why Brits Move to Portugal*, by Lea Melo, "below is a summary of how much it costs per a month to live in one of Portugal's favorite surroundings."

Expenses	Costs*
1 bedroom flat rental	€800
House bills	€120
Groceries	€400
Health insurance	€50 per person
Mobile internet	€20 per person
Transportation (bus + subway)	€40 per person

"Of course, the cost of living varies greatly, depending on the location and one's consumption. However, a couple without children can live very well in Portugal on only €1,500 in monthly expenses."

*Costs are increasing, particularly for housing in Portugal's urban areas, which are higher than areas outside Lisbon.

8. Gastronomy

We admit it. Food is one of the most important aspects of our lives. So when we started to consider places that we could move to, we knew there would have to be good quality food with fresh ingredients and enough variety to keep us interested. Portugal ticks all the boxes.

Incredible fresh seafood and produce, meats, dairy, bread, and bakery items are all plentiful in Portugal. Each region of the country also has its own specialties, making it fun to explore. Everyday restaurants are affordable and delicious, but if we want to splurge on Michelin-starred dining, we have 28 restaurants from which to choose. We won't even go into the phenomenal wine regions here. It's an embarrassment of riches.

A Typical Portuguese Brunch - Timm McBride

There's a reason why Portuguese people spend a lot of time at the table: the best food awaits in every restaurant and tavern! The secret of its richness is in diversity; every region is known for delicious typical dishes with a great offer of meat, fish, seafood, and vegetables that will make you beg for more.

9. Friendliness

Most expats are impressed with the country in general and especially with Porto and Lisbon, which have been rated some of the friendliest cities to live in Europe. We have had wonderful experiences with everyone from rideshare drivers to people we meet randomly at restaurants and walking in the community. There's a special feeling of belonging that comes easily here.

Portugal is Famous for the Seafood - Timm McBride

10. History, Art and Culture

Torre dos Clérigos, Porto - Timm McBride

Did you know that Portugal and Spain have the oldest border in Europe? It dates from 1143 and from then on, history has taken its course in order to transform this country into the greatest place to live. You can find traces of it by visiting the many museums located throughout the country.

Arts and culture abound. No matter what interest we have, there are plenty of places we can go for education, information, entertainment, and sheer pleasure. The architecture is stunning, from churches and historical buildings to palaces and even the tiles on railway stations. Portugal has symphony orchestras, ballet troupes, opera companies, live theaters, and cinemas. It has art museums as well as unique attractions celebrating Portuguese heritage, natural history, science, and even the sea.

Lisbon - The Most Romantic Capital in Europe!

"Seeing Lisbon be considered the most romantic capital in Europe obviously makes us very honoured and confirms what we have been saying in recent years. Lisbon has a wide variety of options for all segments and motivation," says the executive director of Turismo de Lisboa, Paula Oliveira, quoted in a statement to *Notícias ao Minuto.*

Basílica de Estrela, Lisbon - Timm McBride

More and More Americans Wanting to Move to Portugal

"We have a very high demand for visas because we know that Portugal is in fashion and there are more and more Americans or residents in the United States who want to move to Portugal," according to Luisa Pais Lowe, the consul general in New York. "Therefore, we have registered a very large increase in work in the area of visas," she detailed.

The number of North Americans residing in Portugal is at its highest level in more than a decade, according to data from the Foreigners and Borders Service (SEF), cited by Jornal Económico. At the end of 2021, 7,000 people born in the US were living in Portugal, twice as many as during the previous three years. The number of foreigners living in Portugal has increased by 37% since 2011, according to the 2021 censuses released by the National Statistics Institute (INE).

Insider recently featured a Florida man leaving for Portugal because he said rising housing costs, pollution, traffic, and overcrowding have turned his home of 20 years into a rotten paradise.

Portugal is truly a lovely country. Many of us have been unaware of modern Portugal, with our recollection being of historic Portugal based on world history classes from our distant past. Portugal today is a modern, first world country, with many strong reasons to consider it as a viable place to live.

Portuguese Vowel Pronunciation

a (all, ball, fall)   o (lot, not, dog)
e (bet, get, ten)   u (uber, suit, fruit)
i (rico, kilo, diva)   [usually...]

In his recent book, *Should I Move to Portugal?,* Carl Munson notes "Portugal may not quite be heaven on earth, but it's certainly a better place than many others in which to face man-made misery."

CHAPTER 2

COMPARISONS BETWEEN USA AND PORTUGAL

Comparisons between the USA and Portugal are inevitable. Below are a few of the common comparisons data you may be interested in perusing. Much of it is purely academic; other comparisons are more personal and emotional, like health and safety issues. Other issues are more significant to those of us from the US who may want to live here long term; things like national healthcare and other resident benefits.

General comparisons

	USA	Portugal
Year Established	1776	868
Geographic Area	3,796,742 sq mi (9,833,520 km2)	92,212 km2 (35,603 sq mi)
Population	(2020) 331,449,281	(2021) 10,352,042

	USA	Portugal
Currency	US Dollar ($)	Euro (€)
Government	Federal presidential constitutional republic	Unitary semi-presidential constitutional republic
Governmental divisions	50 states, 1 federal district (DC), 5 major unincorporated territories, 9 Minor Outlying Islands, 326 Indian	18 districts of mainland Portugal, divided into 308 municipalities; 2 Atlantic archipelagos of the Azores and Madeira
Political Stability Index world	65	80
Gross Domestic Product/per capita	$25.035 trillion/ $75,180	$432.1 billion/ $42,067
Value Added Tax (VAT)	none (some States have varied sales tax rates)	General 23% Reduced 6-13% Zero 0% (depending on product or service)
Calling code	+ 1	+ 351
ISO 3166 code	US	PT
Internet TLD	.us	.pt
Basic literacy rate	99%	99.4%

	USA	Portugal
College-age citizens who attend higher education institution	52.6%	46.9%
Student loan debt	> 1.7 trillion dollars	(Most student costs are supported with public money)
Quality of life index	170.72	162.52
Crime rates/100,000	Homicide 6.5 Rape 38.4 Robbery 73.9 Aggrav. Assault 279.7 Burglary 314.2 Larceny-Theft 1,398 Motor Veh. theft 246	Murder 0.83 Rape 3.85 (All) Assault 471.57 Dom. violence 218.67
Mass Shootings	(2022) 647 gunviolence.org*	0
Senior discount of travel	10% on some Amtrak fares	50% on monthly transit card, and 50% on intercity train service

Except where noted (*) otherwise, all the above data was extracted from Wikipedia.com.

Comparisons of Labor and Benefits

	USA	Portugal
Mandated minimum wage (varies by State laws)	$7.25 per hour (40 hr/week x 51 weeks = $14,790)	€760 per month (paid 14 times per annum = €10,640/ year)
Average net salary	average $54,132 median $46,625	€14,476
Unemployment rate	(2023) 3.4%	(2023) 6.5%
Mandated bonus pay	[really?]	Mandatory 13th and 14th salary payments, paid out in June for Holidays, and December for Christmas.
Mandated paid vacation	none	22 working days annual leave every calendar year
Mandated paid public holidays	none	13 days per year
Mandated paid family leave	none	30 days of paid leave per year to provide urgent and essential care for a family member younger than 12; and 15 days for an older family member.

	USA	Portugal
Mandated paid maternity leave	none	100.00% of their usual salary rate, paid for by Social Security for 120 days
Mandated paid parental leave	none	For birth of a child, shared between both parents (total parental leave period may be 180 days, paid at 83%. The mother is entitled to 30 days of parental leave before delivery and a minimum of six
Mandated paid paternity leave	[are you kidding?]	Compulsory 20 days, and optional 5 days. Must be taken within 6 weeks of child's birth; minimum of 5 days immediately after birth.
Mandated sick pay	none	Illness <30 days, paid at 55% of the reference remuneration; 31 - 90 days, at 60%; 91 - 365 days, at 70% remuneration.
Mandated marriage leave	[what's that?]	For an employee getting married, 15 consecutive days

	USA	Portugal
Mandated paid family bereavement	none	5 consecutive days

Except where noted (*) otherwise, all the above data was extracted from papayaglobal.com.

Comparisons of Healthcare

	USA	Portugal
CEOWorld Magazine's Health Care Index*	30	22
Healthcare Index numbeo.com*	68.6	71.5
Health Index	71	82
Government health insurance coverage	73%	100%
Life expectancy, male	75 years	78 years
Life expectancy, female	80 years	84 years
Suicide rate - WHO*	16.1	11.5
Obesity rate - Wikipedia*	41.9%	20.8%
Hospital beds per 1000 inhabitants	2.87	3.45
Physicians/1000	2.59	3.34
Diabetes	10.8%	9.8%
HIV	0.20%	0.14%
Smokers	23.0%	25.45%

Except where noted (*) otherwise, all the above data was extracted from www.worlddata.info.

Comparisons of Infrastructure

	USA	Portugal
Roadways/1000 inh	19.85 km	8.03 km
Railways/1000 inch	0.88 km	0.24 km
Waterways/inh	0.12 km	0.02 km
Harbors/1000 inh	0.0109	0.0703
Airports/1000 inh	0.0013	0.0017

All the above data was extracted from www.worlddata.info.

And there's More!

Portugal has so much more to offer. Let's not neglect these other great attractions of Portugal:

Marques de Pombal, Lisbon - Timm McBride

- Virtually limitless historical and natural sights throughout the country, including the islands of Azores and Madeira

- Dozens of celebrated and award winning beaches

- Some of the world's best cities for digital nomads to live and work

- Strong expat/immigrant communities

- World class city centers, as well as enchanting villages and fairytale towns

- Attractive visa programs for expat relocations; one of the most lenient retirement visa applications in Europe

Alfa Pendular flagship high-speed Pendolino tilting train - CP

- Portugal stands out among its counterparts thanks to its sustainable policies on the ecosystem, environment, and people, ranking 16th on the Global Sustainability Index
- Great transportation options throughout the country
- National education system for residents
- Visa-free travel throughout the Schengen Zone
- As a NonHabitual Resident, Portugal has the most favorable tax schemes in the European Union, minimizing your tax liability

CHAPTER 3

TOP CHOICE FOR RETIREES

Enchanting villages and fairytale towns were certainly an attraction for us, as they are for many who choose to move to Portugal. But for day-to-day living, we need access to cosmopolitan cities with lots of amenities in the modern hubbub of life. With three major airports, one in each region, Portugal has accessible and vibrant major cities as well as the charm.

Portugal attracts retirees from around the world, due in part to its low cost of living, warm weather, and rich culture. As a popular retirement location for foreigners, Portugal has a simple, easy visa process for retirees, including qualification for permanent residency or citizenship after five years.

It is critical that all of us, as individuals, consider ways to make our lives more sustainable in order to protect our planet now and in the future. Portugal seems to have achieved this and it's no coincidence that it's the first choice for those who are looking for a more sustainable life.

Portugal provides a stable political and social environment, clear and transparent tax rules, good infrastructure, a favorable investment climate and an excellent quality of life.

Portugal ranked first in the "The World's Best Places to Retire in 2023" in International Living's 2023 Global Retirement Index based on their global sources' experiences. Money.co.uk also ranked Portugal the 2nd healthiest country to live in, with Lisbon coming 3rd out of the top 20 healthiest cities in the world, and Porto in 13th position. "Our mortgage experts rank good food, good company and good transport links being great for the people who live there... Our report is based on life expectancy, the cost to be healthy, air pollution, obesity rates, safety and sunlight hours". What more is there to say?

Portuguese Survival Phrases

Do you speak English?
    Fala Inglés?   (*faa* - la eeng - *glesh*)

I don't understand
    Não entendo (nowng eng - *teng* - doo)

CHAPTER 4

D7 RESIDENCE VISA

The D7 Visa, commonly known as the "Retirement" or "Passive Income" visa was introduced in 2007 by the Portuguese Government. This visa allows non-EU/EEA/Swiss (European Economic Area) citizens to apply for temporary residency in Portugal, based on the applicant having reasonable and regular passive income.

Benefits of the D7 Visa

- Permission to live, work, and/or study in Portugal

- Applicant can extend process for dependent children and dependent parents

- Non visa dependent travel in the Schengen Area

- The opportunity to either establish a business or accept employment in Portugal

- Eventually take advantage of the tax benefits when applying for the Non-Habitual Residency (NHR) scheme

- After a period of five years in which a renewal of visa applications has been followed, the applicant is eligible to qualify for permanent residency or Portuguese citizenship

- Resident rights in Portugal, which include healthcare and education

Requirements for D7 Visa Eligibility

- Applicant must be a Non-EU/EEA/Swiss Citizen
- Proof of funds to be financially self-sustaining during stay in Portugal
- Applicant must have a clean criminal record
- Proof of a residency address in Portugal
- Must spend a minimum of 16 months in Portugal within the first two year period after application

Portuguese Survival Words		
Hello	Olá	(o - *la*)
Goodbye	Adeus	(a - *de* - oosh)
Please	Por favor	(poor fa - *for*)

What Are The Passive Income Requirements

- Documentation of regular passive income from almost any source — social security, bank annuities, military pensions, or private insurance companies, income derived from a pension, rentals, dividend and/or financial investments. Sometimes, applicants can just provide proof of sufficient savings.

- The Portuguese government asks for proof that applicants can financially sustain themselves while living in the country. The amount of income required varies based on factors such as their number of dependents and the Portuguese location where a retiree is planning on living. However, Portugal's general criteria is a minimum monthly income of €700 — roughly $750. (€9.000 per year +50% for a spouse and +30% for each child)

- The applicant should also hold an amount equal to 12 months income in a Portuguese bank account

How at Apply for a D7 Visa

- Applicants must apply for the D7 Visa in their home country, and at their designated Portuguese Consulate. The United States has Portugal Consulates available for visa applications in Washington DC, New York, and San Francisco.

  - Applicant must be physically present in the US when applying for a residency visa for Portugal through the VFS Portugal Visa Application Center.

  - All documents that must be notarized per Embassy checklist should be done by a Notary Public in the state where the applicant legally resides.

  - Check the jurisdiction restrictions before submitting your application at the VFS Visa Application Center. You must apply to the consulate specified on the VFS website according to your current state of residence.

WASHINGTON DC: Alabama, Arkansas, Florida, Georgia, Illinois, Indiana, Iowa, Kansas, Kentucky, Louisiana, Maryland, Minnesota, Mississippi, Missouri, Nebraska, North Carolina, North Dakota, Ohio, Oklahoma, South Carolina, South Dakota, Tennessee, Texas, Virginia, West Virginia, Wisconsin, District of Columbia.

NEW YORK: Connecticut, Michigan and New York, territories of American Virgin Islands, Bahamas, Cayman Islands, and Puerto Rico

SAN FRANCISCO: Alaska, Arizona, California, Colorado, Hawaii, Idaho, Montana, Nevada, New Mexico, Oregon, Utah, Washington and Wyoming

BOSTON: Massachusetts (Counties of: Berkshire, Essex, Franklin, Hampden, Hampshire, Middlesex, Norfolk, Suffolk, Worcester), New Hampshire, Maine and Vermont

- Go to https://visa.vfsglobal.com/usa/en/prt to begin the process of determining the type of visa you will need to apply for, and how to apply. Each Consulate has specific procedures, and may require an in-person visit to apply.

- The Visa Application form is available on the VFS website. A sample of this document can be found in the Appendix section at the end of this book.

- **Fiscal Identification Number (NIF)** A Número de Identificação Fiscal for Portugal (essentially a tax ID number) is a requirement to transact nearly every official process in Portugal. Everything from opening a bank account, to setting up an account with a utility company, to renting or buying a property, requires you to present your Fiscal Number. The two best ways to obtain your NIF from outside Portugal are as follows:

- OPTION 1: For online registration, pay 59€ plus VAT (tax) for this online service at https://www.nifonline.pt/

- OPTION 2: Power of Attorney: You may choose to have a Power of Attorney (POA) drawn. The proxy must be a person who resides in Portugal and has a Taxpayer number. Your proxy will be your Fiscal Representative in Portugal and will be responsible for requesting a Taxpayer number on your behalf. A Portuguese attorney is an excellent resource for this purpose.

- **Accommodation Verification**. Applicants must have a plan as to where they will stay. This can be either a rental property or a purchased property, and it can be located anywhere in the country. Before submitting a formal visa application, individuals can travel to Portugal as tourists and view available properties. Some choose to purchase their own homes, while others opt to rent. Applicants will be expected to provide proof of accommodations for at least a year.

  - Nonresidents are able to purchase property in Portugal, so you may be able to purchase a home anywhere in Portugal to fulfill the accommodation requirement, provided you are able to reside in that property from your intended date of arrival.

- Rental homes are also readily available throughout the country. Multiple websites show rental properties that may be available from various real estate companies and corporate websites, such as Idealista.pt and Apartments.com. There are also rentals available directly from homeowners who, for various reasons, choose to advertise their properties directly on social media sites, such as Facebook Marketplace.

- It is important to make sure that the contract for your rental home is registered with the government Finance department. You will be required to provide documentation with the Finance department registration.

- A third possibility is a Letter of Invitation or Terms of Responsibility. It is a form that can be used as proof of accommodations and/or financial support if you plan to stay with family or friends or are being invited to and sponsored in Portugal by a company or organization.

- **FBI Background Check** is required with the D7 Application, and must be presented either sealed (in the original unopened envelope), or apostilled.* Your fingerprints should

be sent to the FBI for "Identity History Summary Check" processing either electronically or by mail. The results will be mailed to you via US Mail. Visit the FBI website for the most accurate current requirements. https:// www.fbi.gov/services/cjis/identity-history-summary-checks

- At the time of this writing, processing time for Identity History Summary requests submitted electronically is estimated to be three to five business days upon receipt of the fingerprint card. Allow additional time for mail delivery if this option was selected during the request process. Current processing time for Identity History Summary requests submitted via the mail is two to four weeks. Allow additional time for mail delivery.

- The FBI offers three options for requesting your Identity History Summary or proof that one does not exist.

  - OPTION 1: Electronically Submit Your Request Directly to the FBI.

    - Step 1: Go to https://www.edo.cjis.gov.

    - Step 2: Follow the steps under the "Obtaining Your Identity History Summary" section. If you submit a request electronically directly to the FBI, you may visit a participating US Post Office location to submit your fingerprints electronically.

  - OPTION 2: Submit Your Request Directly to the FBI via the Mail

- Step 1: Complete the Applicant Information Form. If the request is for a couple, family, etc., each person must complete and sign a form. Include a complete mailing address, telephone number and e-mail address, if available. Your results will be provided on standard white paper and returned to you by First-Class Mail via the US Postal Service.

- Step 2: Your fingerprints should be placed on a standard fingerprint form (FD-1164) commonly used for applicant or law enforcement purposes.

- Step 3: Submit Payment
    - Payment Option 1: Pay by credit card using the Credit Card Payment Form.

    - Payment Option 2: Obtain a money order or certified check for $18 U.S. dollars made payable to the Treasury of the United States.

- Step 4: Review the Identity History Summary Request Checklist to ensure that you have included everything needed to process your request.

- Step 5: Mail the Required Items Listed Above— signed applicant information form, fingerprint card, and payment of $18 US dollars per person to: FBI CJIS Division – Summary Request

1000 Custer Hollow Road
Clarksburg, WV 26306

- OPTION 3: Submit Your Request to an FBI-Approved Channeler

- An FBI-approved channeler simply helps expedite the delivery of Identity History Summary information on behalf of the FBI. A channeler is a private business that has contracted with the FBI to submit your request on your behalf. FBI-approved Channelers receive the fingerprint submission and relevant data, collect the associated fee(s), electronically forward the fingerprint submission with the necessary information to the FBI for a national Identity History Summary check, and receive the electronic summary check result for dissemination to the individual. My recommendation is to strongly consider this option. Your channeler will be responsible to make sure your FBI Identity History Summary check application is complete and accurate.

- The link on the FBI website lists the FBI-approved channelers: https://www.fbi.gov/services/cjis/identity-history-summary-checks/list-of-fbi-approved-channelers-for-departmental-order-submissions

- **Proof of International Travel Insurance**, including coverage for necessary medical expenses, urgent medical assistance and possible repatriation. Your policy must include the following: Valid for 120 days from the date of travel to Portugal, which is the validity of your visa; No deductible; Minimum €30.000 per person coverage/expenses for which it will pay; Include COVID coverage if you're applying via a VFS Global office; Portugal in the list of countries covered.

- Links to multiple insurance companies that provide these types of insurance are available on the VFS Global website. https://visa.vfsglobal.com/usa/en/prt/travel-insurance

- **The Applicant's Passport**, valid for at least another six months after your relocation. In the event that you would like to retain possession of your passport during the visa application process (such as for interim travel), you may submit a notarized copy of your passport with your visa application. You will then be required to submit the original passport after the visa has been approved, so the visa can be affixed to the passport itself.

- **Itinerary for Outbound Flight** should be provided, showing the visa applicants' names, and flight details,

with airline, flight number, date and time of travel from the US to Portugal. You may have an itinerary for a flight leaving around your intended travel date, yet you don't need to have purchased a ticket.

TAP Air Portugal

- **Personal Statement** declaring the reasons why you are seeking residency in Portugal. The personal statement needs to be clear, concise, and include: a description of yourself, your reason for wanting to move to and reside in Portugal, your ties to Portugal, where you intend to reside initially, what type of accommodations (rental, home purchase) you'll have initially, and how you intend to get money for daily living expenses into Portugal.

- **Portugal Criminal Background Check** form will need to be signed to allow permission to access to the Portuguese criminal record. A sample of this document can be found in the Appendix section at the end of this book.

Practical Tips for Your Visa Application

- *Timing is everything.* Determine when you would like to make your move. Then, plan backwards. The Visa application could, and likely will, take 3 months. VFS recommends NOT applying more than 90 days prior to your intended move date. However, they also warn that the Consulate may take 90 days OR LONGER to approve your application. Be prepared to be flexible!

- You will also be required to have your NIF, Portuguese bank account with funds, accommodation (rental contract), flight reservation, and travel insurance with medical coverage, BEFORE you apply for the Visa. This may seem contrary to our logical way of thinking, however it is the way the system works.

- It may take several weeks, or months, to complete all the preliminary work to apply for your visa. (not to mention that you may need additional time to prepare for your international relocation!) So, flexibility and adjustments may be required in your timeline.

Chapter 7 explains the process for exchanging your US driver license for a new Portuguese driver license. This is not a mandatory process, however, if you intend to drive in Portugal, you will eventually be required to have a Portuguese driver license. It is to your advantage to exchange your US license rather than to re-test in Portugal. In order to take advantage of the exchange process, you must have your certified driver license record apostilled in the state from which it was issued, or the Portuguese consulate. This may be done <u>while you are applying for your visa</u>, eliminating one step in the process.

After completing the application process with the Portuguese Consulate, and receiving your D7 Visa, retirees must travel to Portugal and begin their stay on the temporary resident visa for four months. Within those four months, you should have an appointment with SEF. (Servico de Estrangeiros e Fronteiras) Your Temporary Residence Permits are issued by SEF and are called a Título de Residência. Your first Temporary Residence Permit is valid for two years from the date it is issued and can be renewed for successive periods of three years. These renewals are followed by the option to apply for Permanent Residence or citizenship in the 6th year if you have a certificate of A2 level language proficiency.

For your D7 Visa application, you can expect to pay 90€. You can expect to pay around 160€ for your residence permit.

An <u>apostille</u> authenticates the seals and signatures of officials on public documents such as birth certificates, court orders, marriage license, driver license record, or any other document issued by a government agency or certified by an American or foreign consul. An apostille certifies the document, so the document can be recognized in foreign countries. The apostille must be performed in the same jurisdiction where the document was signed, sealed, or certified (e.g. State of California).

Check the Appendix section at the end of this book for a <u>Checklist</u> for your D7 Application; and a suggested D7 Visa Timeline in Chapter 6.

Portuguese Survival Words

Thank you

Obrigada (female speakers) (o - bree - gaa - da)

Obrigado (male speakers)   (o - bree - gaa - doo)

CHAPTER 5

OTHER VISA OPTIONS

The Portugal Golden Visa - *It's Official: Portugal To End Golden Visa Program*

As reported in *Portugalist.com*, Portugal has announced that it will end its Golden Visa program as it attempts to address the growing lack of affordable property in Portugal. The Golden Visa was introduced in 2012, allowing foreigners to obtain residency by investing in Portugal – most commonly by purchasing a property worth at least €280,000 (but typically €500,000 or more). According to data from SEF data, Portugal issued 11,628 Golden Visas between October 2012 and January 2023.

The announcement on February 16, 2023, follows a comment from the Portuguese Prime Minister, António Costa, made in November stating that the Golden Visa has probably "already fulfilled the function it had to fulfill and which, at this moment, it is no longer justified to maintain."

The D2 Visa - Entrepreneur, Employed and Self-Employed Program exists to attract and fast-track highly qualified, educated professionals to work and invest in Portugal. Highly skilled professionals currently working, or who retired, in the US might follow this approach to start a business or be self-employed in Portugal.

The D6 Family Reunification Visa - There are two visa application options for couples retiring together in Portugal. Both people interested in retiring in Portugal can apply for their own retirement visas (D7), in which case each submits their own separate application. However, if a spouse cannot qualify for any reason, such as a lack of personal income, they can be included as a dependent on the other's visa. This is known as a D6 Visa. An apostilled marriage license is required for a D6 Visa application.

In addition to spouses, applicants can classify parents and any minor children, as well as children over 18 who are attending a school in Portugal, as dependents. In order to include dependents, an applicant must prove they have sufficient income to provide for everyone, as well as accommodations for all.

Portuguese Survival Phrase

Where's the toilet?

Onde é a casa de banho?

(*ong* - de e a *kaa* - za de *ba* - nyoo)

The D1 Visa - Subordinate worker visa. For a person to be eligible for D1 Visa, he/she must have recently received a job offer in Portugal. The D1 Visa is valid for immigrants with a job contract that lasts for at least 12 months.

The D4 Student VISA is available with requirements similar to the D7, documentation confirming educational enrollment, and type of study.

New VISA Options: As of October 30, 2022, the Portuguese government implemented new measures to simplify immigration procedures, will especially target the Community of Portuguese Language Countries (CLP) (Brazil, Angola, Cabo Verde, Guinea-Bissau, Equatorial Guinea, Mozambique, Portugal, Sao Tome and Principe, and Timor-Leste), digital nomads, and researchers.

Specifically, nationals of CPLP members can apply for granting and renewal of residence permits in Portugal without having to submit proof of valid travel insurance, evidence or means of subsistence, or a copy of the return ticket. In addition, these travelers will be enabled to apply online for these services without having to be present when filing for a visa.

The Job Seeker Visa for employment search. As stated in its name, it will be suitable for those searching for a job. Temporary stay visas allow entry and stay in Portugal for less than a year. Temporary stay visas are valid during the entire stay and allow for multiple entries. Here is a list of the documents that will help you to get it:

- Proof of three minimum monthly salaries
- Declaration of conditions of stay

- Evidence of submission of a declaration of interest for admission at IEFP (Portuguese Institute of Employment and Training).

The visa mentioned here will be valid for 120 days. However, you have a chance to extend it for sixty more days. A request for an extension has to be complemented by evidence of IEFP enrollment, and it is effective only within the territory of Portugal.

D8 Digital Nomad Visa There are two types of Digital Nomad Visas: Temporary Stay Visa or D7 Residence Visa. The Digital Nomad Temporary Stay Visa it is valid for up to one year, allowing you to stay in Portugal, with the possibility of extension for the same period. In addition to the requirements common to the other visas, the "digital nomad" options have the following requirements.

- In case of subordinate work, one of the following documents:
  - Work contract, or
  - Declaration by employer confirming the employment contract
- In case of independent professional activity, one of the following documents:
  - Society contract, or
  - Contract of services provision, or
  - Document attesting the services provided to one or more entities
- Proof of average monthly income for the last three months with a minimum value equivalent to four monthly

minimum guaranty remuneration. *(at least €2,800 per month - four times Portugal's minimum wage)*

- Document attesting fiscal residence

The referenced documents are the mandatory initial documents to be submitted. The consular post may request additional documents, at their discretion.

Other Visa Options are available for specific purposes. Check the Portuguese Consulate (https://vistos.mne.gov.pt/en/) and VFS (https://www.vfsglobal.com/one-pager/portugal/usa/english/) websites for more details.

CHAPTER 6

D7 VISA TIMELINE

O btaining your D7 Visa(s) can be a daunting process. But with a little planning, and some organization, you should be able to complete this task with only a moderate degree of anxiety. It is essential to follow <u>all</u> the steps <u>exactly</u> to be certain that you meet the requirements of VFS and the Consulate. Stories of people who tried to shortcut the system in various ways, only to have their applications denied, are very disheartening.

You will likely need to allow about eight months to complete the process, from your initial contacts with an attorney, opening a bank account and applying for a NIF; and your actual move date. The following is an approximation of our timeline when we decided to relocate from California to Lisbon in August 2021.

Always check with Embassy and VFS immediately prior to your application visit to verify *exact* fees. Money orders must be for the *exact* amounts owed that day.

D7 VISA TIMELINE

Timeline	Essential Action	Recommended	Optional
- 8 mo			Hire attorney * (4300€ x 50%)
- 8 mo	Apply for NIF		
- 8 mo	Open bank account		
- 7 mo	Fingerprints, apply for FBI report (valid for 6 months)		
- 5 mo	Make appt with VFS to apply for visa		
- 5 mo	Contract for rental apartment (€1100 x 2 mo rent; plus €1100 x 6 mo deposit)		
- 4 mo	Deposit to bank account for 2 adults (€9,120 x 1.5)		
- 4 mo	Arrange flights	Purchase airfare	
- 4 mo	Purchase flight & medical insurance		
- 4 mo	Write cover letter(s)		
- 3 mo	Money orders to Embassy and VFS		
- 3 mo	Apply for D7 visa		
- 2 mo		Arrangements for shipping and insurance of household goods	
- 1 mo			Make airline reservation for pet

Timeline	Essential Action	Recommended	Optional
- 1 mo			Make vet appointment(s) for pet travel
- 1 mo		Obtain (2) state certified copies of driver licenses	Submit to consulate for authentication
- 1 mo			Utility applications and connections
- 1 mo		Book transportation from airport to your new	
- 10 days			Pet exam by US vet
- 10 days			Submit documentation to FDA for pet travel
- 1 week		Reserve and pay airline for excess luggage	
- 3 days			Receive USDA certificate for pet
- 2 days			Email pet travel documents to PT airport vet
Day 0	Flight(s) to Portugal	Save boarding passes & luggage claim tickets	Visit with PT airport vet prior to entering Customs
+ 1 mo		Apply for SNS Health Service	
+ 1 mo		Apply for Mass Transit card	

Timeline	Essential Action	Recommended	Optional
+ 3 mo	SEF Appointment to finalize Residency		Pay attorney balance (4300€ x 50%) Attorney may attend this visit *
+ 3 mo			Driver License exchange

CHAPTER 7

DRIVER LICENSE EXCHANGE

The IMT (Instituto da Mobilidade e dos Transportes), which is the authority that issues driver licenses in Mainland Portugal has a process by which an immigrant (that's you!) can exchange a foreign driver license for a Portuguese driver license. You can follow the process online at www.imtonline.pt.

The Basic Rules are as Follows:

You can drive in Portugal, as a tourist, with a driver license issued by the US, for a period of 185 days following your entry into Portugal and providing you are not intending to settle.

If you take up residence in Portugal, you must take into account the following deadlines, which are effective from the date on which your residence document is issued:

- Up to 90 days. You can continue to drive on a license issued by the US for up to 90 days from the date of issue of your residence document, but you must apply to IMT for an exchange during this period.

- From 90 days up to 2 years. You can no longer drive on a license issued by the US, but you can still apply to IMT for an exchange during this period.

- After 2 years. You can apply for the exchange of your license, but you will have to pass a practical driving test in Portuguese.

What do I Need to do to Exchange my Driving License?

First, you must be an official resident of Portugal with a valid residence permit/card issued by SEF (no, your D7 visa is not enough... you must have the residence permit/card), a NIF issued by Finanças, a Portuguese bank account from which to make the electronic payment, and a Número de Utente issued by SNS (National Health Service).

Start by asking your Portuguese doctor for a medical exam. After the exam, the doctor will issue a medical certificate and send it electronically to IMT via the medical certificate platform. Then:

- The license exchange process must be initiated online. Access, fill out and submit with the following documents: (exception: residents of the Azores or Madeira must contact their local driving authority for instructions).

- Residence permit, from SEF

- Certificate of Authenticity of the driving license, issued by the issuing entity or consular service, indicating the categories obtained by examination (and what type of test) and the categories obtained by equivalence. This may be accomplished by having your US certified driver license record apostilled in the state from which it was issued, or the Portuguese consulate. Check with *your* consulate for their specific requirements. The certification must be carried out by the Portuguese Consulate or the consular services of another member state in the respective country of origin.

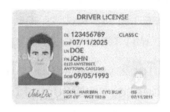

- Foreign Driver license (to be relinquished to IMT)

- A psychological assessment certificate, <u>if you are applying to retain vehicle categories C, D and/or E</u>

After submitting the request, you must wait for communication from IMT with an indication to go to the IMT service desk.

Yes, this is a tedious process, but it allows eligible drivers to exchange their license without having to test in Portuguese.

<table>
<tr><td colspan="2" align="center">**Portuguese Survival Phrase**</td></tr>
<tr><td>**You're welcome**</td><td>**De nada**   **(de *na* - da)**</td></tr>
</table>

New Driver License Exchange Rules

as reported in Portugal News 12 July 2022:

New rules allow for drivers with licenses from states with a bilateral agreement with the Portugal to be officially recognized. The United States is recognized under this rule.

According to the amendment published in the Diário da República, the exchange of driving licenses has been waived, "enabling driving in the national territory with titles issued in those States, through the recognition of foreign driving titles."

This recognition applies to driver's licenses <u>if no more than 15 years have elapsed since the issue or the last renewal and provided that the holder is less than 60 years of age.</u> These rules would obviously preclude many of us from qualifying, and will still require exchanging our US driver licenses to continue to drive in Portugal.

Note: An "International Driving Permit" is not required in Portugal, nor does it help you in any way to comply with or extend or skirt any of the time limitations described.

CHAPTER 8

FINDING A NEW HOME

Finding a new home in an unfamiliar country is certainly a daunting challenge! But, it is not insurmountable. I recommend that you first decide in which area you would like to live, and the type of environment (urban, rural, etc.) and the type of residence in which you would like to live. (multi-family apartment, single family villa, farm) And of course, whether you plan to rent or intend to purchase a property. It is advisable to strongly consider renting a home at first if you are not certain of the area in which you would like to reside. Many expats rent for a year or two, then look for a property to purchase, which gives you the time to make sure you end up locating in the area in which you really want to stay.

Homes come in many shapes and sizes, just like in other parts of the world. You are probably familiar with single-family homes, townhomes, condominiums, multifamily apartment buildings, and perhaps other types of dwellings.

Portugal, likewise, has various types of residential buildings. some of the most common are multi-family buildings with commercial or retail spaces on the ground floor, and upper floors comprised of residential units. And, of course, single family homes on residential lots are available in many areas, usually outside the city centers. These are called villas in Portugal.

Buildings in Portugal. Yes, there are a lot of buildings in Portugal: new, old, and very old! Many are so old they survived the epic Lisbon earthquake of 1755! Generally, you will find that buildings, especially of the modern era, are well constructed with thick solid exterior walls and tile roofs. They also tend to have smaller windows than we may be accustomed to, in order to minimize heat gain and loss.

Heating and Air Conditioning. Most homes are built without central heat or AC; but many have been retrofitted with "split systems" which are quite common throughout Europe. These heat pumps consist of an externally installed compressor, and one or more interior mounted condensers that distribute heated/cooled air throughout the interior rooms. Portable heat pumps and various types of electric heaters are also readily available for temporary installation, and are ideal for rental apartments for a quick, inexpensive solution for your home.

Home Appliances. As we have learned, all home appliances are 240 VAC, and a rental apartment is not likely to be equipped with heat/AC, most apartments are also rented with only a kitchen cooktop/stove (called a "hob" here), an extractor fan (range hood fan), and a water heater. These heating appliances may be either gas or electric, usually depending on the availability of natural gas to the building. You may notice I also left out refrigerator, dishwasher, washer, and dryer. I also excluded garbage disposal. *Nobody* has a garbage disposal here. (Well, I do know of one.) This may necessitate buying all these appliances yourself to furnish your new home.

A Typical Residential Neighborhood in Almada - Timm McBride

Be sure to check whether your new home has a space and electrical connection for a clothes dryer. They are actually uncommon here in Portugal. That's what clothes lines are for — and they are everywhere! Clean and efficient laundromats are available in most neighborhoods with large capacity, high efficiency machines for those without in-home laundry facilities.

Renting an Apartment. This is probably the most common means of establishing a home in Portugal when arriving for your residency. Searching for available homes to rent or purchase is not as simple as you may want it to be. Unlike in the US, there is no unified "multiple listing service" (MLS). However, there are some useful internet sites to help you with your search. One commonly used site is https://www.idealista.com/. Private real estate company websites are also very useful when searching for available homes. RE/MAX and Century 21 both have strong presences in Portugal.

Be Prepared for some unusual rental terms when renting in Portugal. It is not unusual for landlords to require expats to pay 2 months' rent as security deposit, plus six months or more rent in advance in order to secure a rental contract. *Remember - you are a foreigner here.* And you will be required to present a valid rental contract in order to apply for your visa. A valid contract will be signed by the landlord and the renter, and be registered with the Finance Department. Do not neglect the last requirement; it is what makes your rental contract valid! Do not accept a rental contract from an unregistered property.

Another rather unusual feature of home rental contracts in Portugal is that you may terminate the contract after having fulfilled 1/3 of its term. That's only four months of a 12-month term. After that period, you are required to give proper notice (registered mail) to vacate in 120 days. This allows you to relocate if you find a more permanent home during the initial term of your rental contract.

Buying a Home in Portugal can be a relatively simple process; it can also be a very complicated process. Assuming you find a property you would like to purchase, (and it is properly register as a residence, and it is owned by a willing seller), purchasing is straightforward. Sometimes, properties are owned by multiple family members who do not agree on the price and terms of a sale, making a sale impossible. Do your best to avoid this situation.

Portuguese banks also make relatively inexpensive mortgage loans to expats, usually with a 30% cash down payment. The term of the loan may depend on the age of the borrowers. Banks typically do not loan beyond the borrower's 75th year. So if you're 65 years old, that's a 10 year mortgage. Sometimes they make exceptions.

When purchasing a property in Portugal, you will be expected to pay not only the required cash down payment, but also the taxes, insurance, and all other necessary fees in cash at the time of the transaction (closing). These costs will not be "rolled into" your mortgage. Likewise, there is no escrow fund with which the bank will pay future insurance and taxes from. You will be personally responsible for those as well.

Portuguese Survival Phrases

Greetings are important. Preface every transaction with "Bom dia" or "Boa tarde."

Good morning	Bom dia	(bong *dee* - a)
Good afternoon	Boa trade	(*bo* - a *tar* - de)
Good evening	Boa noite	(*bo* - a *noy* - te)

Whether You Rent or Buy, the assistance of a qualified real estate professional and/or attorney is highly advisable. All the paperwork and contracts will be in Portuguese and your professionals will help protect your interests in the transaction.

CHAPTER 9

WHAT SHOULD I TAKE WITH ME?

There is no easy, one-size-fits-all answer to this question. It is different for everyone. Some people want to take all their worldly possessions — which is very difficult — and expensive. Others want to leave all the "stuff" behind, make a clean break and start over in a new country.

Most of us have lots of "stuff." And most of us don't need all that "stuff." As you look around you to start the task of deciding what to keep and take with you, and what you can let go of, you will likely realize that most of the "stuff" does not need to go with you.

Having just recently gone through that process of purging ourselves of the "stuff," a statement I saw in another expat's post became very obvious: "As you purge, purge, and purge again, it becomes crystal clear that *stuff is the enemy of freedom.*"

In many cases, your personal items can be more easily and inexpensively replaced than transported abroad.

To be clear, each person will devise their own system of separating their worldly possessions into their own classifications, based on their own values and sentiments.

As I write this, I wonder why anyone else would want to listen to *my* opinion about what *they* should keep, or get rid of, or take halfway around the world to their new home. Well, we did recently complete this exercise ourselves, and I think I may have a few worthwhile pointers on the subject.

"Do you want to change where you live, or do you want to change your life?" my husband has frequently asked of others seeking guidance regarding what to bring, and how to prioritize the bringing of their stuff. Is it your desire to simply transfer your current life into another location, or is it your goal to begin an exciting new life in a fantastic new place?

Do you want to keep the same house, furniture, cars, and other belongings — only in another place? Or are you willing to "give up" many of your familiar possessions in order to discover an entirely new way of living? Perhaps you will be moving from an urban city environment to a more relaxed, slower paced community away from the cities, or to a coastal region, or to the mountains.

There is a lot to be said, learned, and even gained, by relinquishing the familiar, for the new and unfamiliar. Your life will be different whatever you decide, because you cannot really just relocate your entire life halfway around the world. It is inherently a different lifestyle.

And so it goes, how to decide what to do with all the things we have spent so many years accumulating — all the things we surround ourselves with that bring us comfort. It's probably a good time to try to understand why we have collected all the stuff we have collected, and how we can come to live without most of it.

We chose to move to Lisbon, the capital city of Portugal. It offered an urban environment, with a high population density, cobblestone streets and sidewalks, to live in a smaller apartment, on a subway line, surrounded by graffiti, small shops, restaurants, fruit markets. And a wonderful community of delightful people infinitely patient with our flailing attempts at speaking Portuguese.

We *decided* we would be satisfied living here without many of the niceties we had become accustomed to — the nice big house, pool, spa, electric cars, grand piano, and fenced yard, in a gated community. We left all that, all our furniture, and virtually all our worldly possessions behind, for a *new life in a new country*.

Do not misunderstand, there is nothing wrong with bringing your stuff — and we did bring some stuff — you just have to decide what is important to you, weighing the costs of bringing it and the value of having it here with you.

There are multiple methods of bringing your belongings with you. Keep in mind, however, that you are only able to ship into the country one shipment of household goods within the first year of your arrival without taxation, so it is imperative to get it right the first time! In any case, all household goods shipped into the country that are less than one year old may be subject to taxation, so don't go out and buy all new computers, cellphones, etc., just before you move.

It was during this process that I discovered a book written by an elderly woman, titled *Dostadning - The Swedish Art of Death Cleaning*, by Margareta Magnusson.

> From the Amazon profile: *In Sweden there is a kind of decluttering called döstädning, dö meaning "death" and städning meaning "cleaning." This surprising and invigorating process of clearing out unnecessary belongings can be undertaken at any age or life stage but should be done sooner than later, before others have to do it for you. In The Gentle Art of Swedish Death Cleaning, artist Margareta Magnusson, with Scandinavian humor and wisdom, instructs readers to embrace minimalism. Her radical and joyous method for putting things in order helps families broach sensitive conversations, and makes the process uplifting rather than overwhelming.*
>
> *Margareta suggests which possessions you can easily get rid of (unworn clothes, unwanted presents, more plates than you'd ever use) and which you might want to keep (photographs, love letters, a few of your children's art projects). Digging into her late husband's tool shed, and her own secret drawer of vices, Margareta introduces an element of fun to a potentially daunting task. Along the way readers get a*

glimpse into her life in Sweden, and also become more comfortable with the idea of letting go.

In short, it is a charming, practical, and unsentimental approach to putting a home in order while reflecting on the tiny joys that make up a long life. Her insights were invaluable during this process.

In short, we classified everything into four basic categories:

1. What <u>absolutely has to go with us</u> - things we cannot live without. Items that were irreplaceable, too valuable to let go, or a must-have for our new home in Portugal!

2. What we can easily <u>get rid of</u> - stuff of little value, had outlived its usefulness, or could be donated to a charity.

3. What has significant value, <u>to be sold</u> - to help offset the costs of taking the essential stuff with us.

4. <u>Sentimental items</u> - family heirlooms, valuable gifts, that cannot be taken with us. These treasures will be passed on to family members, friends, or given/sold to someone who will appreciate it.

Please keep in mind that there are some personal items that are just not worth taking to Portugal. Most of your electric and electronic devices cannot be used in Portugal. The power system is 240VAC, 50Hz; the US power system is 120/240VAC, 60Hz. Most of our electrical appliances are completely incompatible with Portugal's power system.

Many new electronics, however, are multi-voltage (120-240VAC, 50-60Hz) such as all modern Apple® computers, tablets, and cellphones. See Chapter 12 on electrical devices for a more complete description of what works and what doesn't.

Many people also question whether taking their car is worthwhile. In most cases, shipping your car is not worth the expenses, which include modifications necessary to meet EU standards, and taxes and fees. Chapter 10 will detail the pros and cons of different automotive options.

How to take our furry four-legged family members is another common question; they also deserve a chapter unto themselves; see Chapter 13. Most of us wouldn't leave home without them!

First, you are allowed to check numerous bags on the airline with you when you fly over. We checked 11 bags without any difficulty. Look into upgrading your airfare to include as many checked bags as possible; it's probably less expensive than paying for 'extra' checked bags. Nevertheless, you will

likely check 'extra' bags for additional fees. Be sure to notify the airline in advance and pay for those extra checked bags prior to your arrival to the airport on the day of departure.

Inexpensive "Heavy Duty Extra Large Moving Bags W/ Backpack Straps Strong Handles & Zippers" are readily available from Amazon. They worked great for this purpose.

Another common method of shipping personal items is on pallets. This service is available from multiple shipping companies, including at least one that will deliver their pallet(s) to your home, that you pack yourself. They then pick up your pallets and and ship them overseas. The pallets are 48" x 48" and vary in height from about three to seven feet, so you can assemble, mix, and match pallets as

needed to ship the personal items you choose. These can be delivered directly to your door at your new home in Portugal! Although much less costly than a full size shipping container, the costs do add up, especially with recommended insurance.

There is also the option of packing and shipping a partial or entire 40 foot shipping containers, for those who

Timm McBride

Page 74

choose to bring more and larger quantities of household goods.

Household goods shipped into Portugal need to be inventoried and a Luggage Certificate obtained from a Portuguese consulate in the US. If you use a commercial shipper, they will help ensure that the requirements are met. In some cases, depending on the route of entry into the EU, a simple certification by you will suffice, if none of your household items are less than six months old.

ITEMS SUBJECT TO DUTIES AND/OR RESTRICTIONS

- New items (less than six months old) or items not showing obvious signs of use (packing in the manufacturer's original cartons is not recommended)

- Electrical appliances and electronic items must be shown on the inventory with make, model, serial number and value.

- Tobacco products

- Antiques (provenance showing more than 100 years old) (Above items should be loaded near container doors for easy access by Customs)

- A reasonable quantity of wine and spirits in a household goods import equivalent to the contents of a normal domestic wine rack and cocktail cabinet

PROHIBITED ITEMS

- Narcotics/illegal drugs of any kind

- Pornography and subversive material

- Games of chance and any gambling paraphernalia

- Gold bars & systems for counterfeiting Portuguese postage stamps

- Perishable foodstuffs

- Apes & monkeys, any animal on the Endangered Species List and some dog breeds

- Firearms and corresponding ammunition up to caliber 7.62mm is allowed with a permit issued by Portuguese authorities. ALL other explosives, weapons, ammunitions and war instruments are strictly prohibited.

Luggage Certificate from a Portuguese Consulate in US

The purpose of this document is to help you request a luggage certificate so that you don't get taxed for bringing items you've owned for six months or more.

Information is accurate as of July 2022)—please confirm by visiting https://saofrancisco.consuladoportugal.mne.gov.pt/en/consular-matters/consular-services/luggage-certificate

Required documents:

- Signed and dated Declaration (must be in Portuguese, see example). Add two copies of the Declaration (The original, plus two copies. The copies do not need to be notarized)

- Include three copies of the list of goods

Portuguese Survival Phrase

My name is ...

O meu nome é ...   **(oo *me* - oo *no* - me e ...)**

- Copy of valid Portuguese ID Card OR copy of valid Portuguese Passport, or third country Passport (personal data page)

- Proof of US residency (for example: US driver's license or utility bill)

- Cover letter explaining the service you require and your contacts (email and cellphone number)

- Self-addressed postmarked envelope, with a minimum size of 10x13

- Check payable to "Portuguese Consulate." *The amount changes, so go to the following link, click on the "Consular Fees" link, and look for Certificates.* *https://saofrancisco.consuladoportugal.mne.gov.pt/en/consular-matters/consular-fees*

Write a short cover letter explaining the service you require, with your email address and cellphone number. Here's an example:

> *Dear Sir or Madam,*
>
> *Enclosed please find the documents and payment necessary for the luggage certificate. We will be leaving to Portugal on [date].*
>
> *My email address is [emailaddress@email.com]*
>
> *My mobile number is [(818)555-1234]*
>
> *Our address is: [123 Street Name, City, State Zip]*
>
> *Thank you so much for your attention.*

A sample of this document can be found in the **Appendix** section at the end of this book.

Portuguese Survival Numbers

0	zero (ze - roo)	6	seis (saysh)
1	um (oong)	7	sete (se - te)
2	dois (doysh)	8	oito (oy - too)
3	três (treze)	9	nove (no - ve)
4	quatro (kwaa - troo)	10	dez (desh)
5	cinco (seeng - koo)	100	sem (seng)

CHAPTER 10

SHOULD I TAKE MY CAR?

Cars and motorcycles that have been in the customer's possession for at least six months can be imported duty-free. They must meet EU standards, which may require mechanical work before they are shipped. Duty and tax will be applied on all newly purchased cars. The duty and

tax rates vary based on year, make, model, and engine size. The duty and tax rates are very high.

Documentation needed:

- Original of the vehicle registration in your name
- Title
- International driver's license
- Insurance document

One vehicle may be imported duty-free every five years. If you sell the vehicle within the first 12 months after importing it, you will be charged the full amount of *Imposto Sobre Veiculos* (ISV) that you would have paid; however after 12 months, you may sell it without any charge.

After the vehicle is imported, you have 180 days in which to register your vehicle and receive Portuguese license plates, at which time the ISV is charged. The vehicle must also be inspected and be brought into compliance with Portuguese highway standards, which vary depending on the make, model, and age of the vehicle. The inspection may be done at any authorized inspection center within the country. There are different rules for classic or collectible cars, however, any car that conforms to EU standards will pass the Portuguese inspection.

Step-by-step to Importing Your Car to Portugal

Here are the steps you'll need to follow to import a car to Portugal:

1. Compile all your documents
2. Access Portal das Finanças
3. Have the Certificate of Conformity (COC) in your hands
4. Print the IMT Model 9 form
5. Fill out the Customs declaration form (DAV)
6. Pay the DUC (Documento Único de Cobrança)
7. Book an inspection after the vehicle arrives
8. Pay remaining taxes (VAT and ISV)
9. Get the Documento Único Automóvel
10. Register your car and get the license plates

Do I Need to Have a Car in Portugal?

Many people have chosen to live a simpler lifestyle when moving to Portugal. This sometimes means *not* owning a car at all. Transportation is readily available in the urban areas; and train and bus services crisscross the entire country. You may find it liberating to not own a car — we have! Check out Chapter 11 on public transportation for more details on how we get by *without* a car.

What Type of Car Should I Drive in Portugal?

You have as many options in Portugal as you do in the US, new or used, gasoline, diesel, electric, and hybrids. Just note that fuels are generally more expensive in Portugal than in the US. That goes for both electricity and fossil fuels.

The ongoing debate about whether to purchase a new vehicle or a used one continues with the same pros and cons we are already familiar with. A new car will cost more to purchase, but will probably require less maintenance, be more reliable, and likely be more fuel efficient than a used

---

Portuguese Survival Phrases

Call the police
Chame a polícia
(*shah* - me a poo - *lee* - sya)

I need a doctor
Eu preciso de um médico
(*e* - oo pre - *see* - zoo de oong *me* - dee - koo)

---

car. Used cars may cost less, but will likely require increased maintenance and repairs, and may also be less fuel efficient.

Also, for simply practical reasons, as a newcomer to the country, and probably not having an adequate grasp of the Portuguese language, buying a used car could be more daunting and potentially risky.

In Portugal, vehicle types and fuel varieties rival the selection in the US, with one big exception: You will see virtually no large cars or trucks, nor are you likely to need or want one. The streets are generally narrower, parking is limited — especially in urban areas. And fuel costs make most large vehicles impractical.

Diesel (gasoleo) is a popular fuel for passenger cars, as well as trucks, and is readily available. Diesel powered cars have been common in Europe for decades, and are well refined and common in even the most expensive luxury models. Gasoline (gasolina) powered cars are also available in many models. Incidentally, most passenger cars are equipped with manual transmissions, so if this is a major concern, your search for your ideal car with an automatic transmission may be tedious. Better yet, brush up on your shifting skills.

Hybrid and electric vehicles are also becoming quite popular in Portugal, and several manufacturers, including several not represented in the US, offer numerous hybrid and electric variants.

Peugeot, Skoda, Opel, Citroen, and Seat are some of the common manufacturers of passenger vehicles available, in addition to brands that are more familiar to North American drivers: Toyota, Nissan, Honda, Hyundai, Fiat, Smart, Mercedes, BMW, Jaguar, Volkswagen, Ford, Tesla, and Porsche, and more.

The Portugal News reported on 3 April, 2023 that the first electric vehicles will be manufactured in Portugal by Stellantis, with the company revealing that from 2025 battery electric light commercial vehicles will be produced at its factory located in Mangualde.

Mangualde will therefore be the first Portuguese industrial unit to produce fully electric battery cars, for the domestic and export markets.

The 100% electric models to be produced in Mangualde are the Citroën ë-Berlingo, Peugeot e-Partner, Opel Combo-e and Fiat e-Doblò, in light commercial and passenger versions.

CHAPTER 11

TRANSPORTATION OPTIONS

Historic Lisbon Eléctrico #28 - Carris

Public transportation can be a dirty word for some people. The thought of boarding a dirty old rickety bus with a bunch of strangers may not be appealing. The reality, however, is quite a different picture. Mass transit options in the urban areas are abundant: subway, urban and intercity buses, streetcar, funicular, ferry, and regional and intercity trains. Then there are always taxis, and Uber and Bolt options, not to mention numerous rentable bicycles and scooters.

CP (Comboios de Portugal) is a state-owned company operating passenger trains in Portugal. In 2019, transported 145 million passengers, over approximately 3,500 km (2,000 mi) of railway. CP is split into three divisions:

- CP Longo Curso, long-distance mainline services (Alfa Pendular, Intercidades and International trains).

- CP Regional, regional services (Interregional and Regional).

- CP Urban Services
  - CP Lisboa, Lisbon's suburban network.
  - CP Porto, Porto's suburban network.
  - CP Coimbra, Coimbra's suburban network.

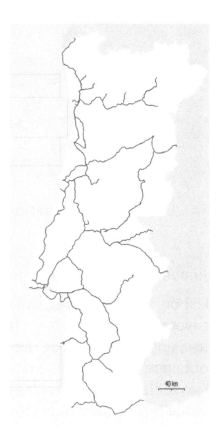

CP Rail Map

Lisbon Metro Map

When we moved over here, it was our decision to live in an urban area within the mass transit system specifically to avoid needing to buy a car. Now that's not to say we will never buy a car, but it is our goal. (Perhaps a scooter will be a compromise that will allow a little more personal transportation freedom without the "inconvenience" and expense of car ownership)

Lisbon, Porto, and perhaps other populous areas, offer several transit cards and passes, for single-use, short-term use, and long-term use. As long-term residents, we obtained monthly reloadable passes that include unlimited transport on all the modes in the Lisbon region, allowing us virtually unlimited travel throughout the area. Other areas have similar plans.

Lisbon Navegante regional transit pass	Monthly
Navegante Metropolitano (adult)	€40

Lisbon Navegante regional transit pass	Monthly
Navegante Municipal (adult)	€30
Navegante +65 (senior)	€20
Navegante Família Metropolitano	€80
Navegante Família Municipal	€60

Lisbon has recently added *free* Navegante Municipal service for Seniors! And Senior Citizens (Aged 65 years or older) are also entitled to other transportation discounts: 25%

Ferry between Lisbon and Cacilhas - TTSL

discount on Navegante Rede and Intermodal passes; and 60% on Navegante Urbano.

The city and intercity buses are all very modern, clean, and well maintained. The schedules are published, with regular service, and arrival times available via SMS (text) at designated stops. Many of our trips within the city are a combination of Metro subway, bus, and/or ferry, with overall good efficiency.

In addition to an efficient taxi system, Uber and Bolt offer a robust fleet of cars and vans operated by independent drivers who provide quick hassle-free transport through all the areas of the country we have visited. Uber and Bolt have become our regular backup whenever we need a ride home from the grocery store, or out to an area without regular bus service. Lisbon also has several vendors that provide access to short-term scooter and bicycle rentals throughout the city.

BIRD Rentable Electric Scooter

TAP Air Portugal is the state-owned flagship airline of Portugal, headquartered at Lisbon Airport which also serves as its hub. TAP has been a member of the Star Alliance since

Portugal International Airports

2005 and operates on average 2,500 flights a week to 90 destinations, in 34 countries worldwide. Portugal has three international airports: Porto, Lisbon, and Faro.

Portuguese Survival Words		
bus	autocarro	(ow - to kaa - roo)
train	comboio	(kong - *boy* - oo)
boat	barco	(*baar* - koo)
tram	eléctrico	(e - *le* - tree - koo)
airport	aeroporto	(a - e - ro - *por* - too)

CHAPTER 12

ABOUT ELECTRICAL APPLIANCES

Electrical appliances can be of special concern when your destination country utilizes a different electrical system than your home country.

The typical family uses dozens of electrical devices in our homes, and we are usually relatively oblivious to their electrical requirements. We just plug them in and use them.

Things are not that simple when we move to a new country that uses a different power system. To begin with, let's assume that *none* of our devices will function in Portugal; then we'll look at exceptions to that rule.

Let's discuss the differences between the US and Portuguese electrical systems. The obvious difference is that the outlets and plugs are different. And there are good reasons for that.

The US employs a combination of 110 (110-120) volt and 220 (220-240) volt devices for household use. **Voltage** (V) is the difference difference of electric potential (electromotive force) between two points, measured in **volts**.

US residential electrical power is **alternating current** (AC), an electric current that continuously reverses direction at 60 cycles per second (Hertz, **Hz**). Portuguese electrical systems use 50 Hz AC.

> The amount of current, commonly referred to as "power consumption" is measured in **amperes** (amps, **A**), and is sometimes expressed in **milliamps**, 1/000 amp (**mA**). **Wattage** is also a unit of measurement used to determine the amount of energy. It is calculated by multiplying amps by voltage, and is expressed in **watts** (**W**).

The major differences between US and Portuguese electrical power systems are voltage and Hertz. US uses **110 volts AC, 60 Hz**, for most household devices (except major appliances like water heater, electric heat, air conditioning, electric dryer, range, and oven); and Portugal uses **240 volts AC, 50 Hz**. The outlets for portable electrical devices in the US is the familiar double straight blade outlet (with or without a ground hole). For Portugal there are two associated plug types, C and F. Plug type C is the plug which has two round pins, and type F has two round pins with two earth clips on the side, both 240 VAC, 50 Hz.

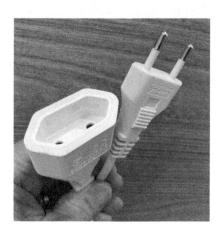

Ungrounded and Grounded Receptacles and Plugs

While adapters are available to connect your 110 VAC plugs into these outlets, if your device is not compatible with 240 VAC, 50 Hz, your electrical appliance will be damaged, and likely beyond repair!

Appliances with lights, motors, and heaters designed for 110 VAC will likely be destroyed by the increased "electromotive force" of 240 VAC. Voltage converters are available which may allow operation of some appliances by reducing the voltage to 110 VAC, however, operation of a motorized appliance designed to function on 60 Hz will run slower on 50 Hz.

Now for the Good News! You probably have some devices that are designed to operate satisfactorily on Portugal's "higher power." Many newer electronic devices, particularly those which are rechargeable and powered by plug-in adapters. Rechargeable razors, clippers, cellphones, tablets, and laptop computers often have dual-voltage adapters rated at 110-240 VAC, 50-60 Hz. Look closely at the fine print on the transformer; if you see this language, you're good to go. All you will need is a simple adapter to plug into the 240 V outlet.

Electrical Specifications Label (100-240 VAC — 50-60 Hz)

Don't worry about leaving behind your beloved small appliances. Europe, and Portugal in particular, has an enormous variety of high-quality appliances at affordable prices. You can buy anything you need when you land here!

Simple 120 V to 240 V plug adapter

One pleasant surprise we had when we bought new furniture and appliances in Portugal is the guarantee for products purchased in Portugal. According to portugal.gov.pt, "Any product purchased in Portugal has a mandatory guarantee period during which the consumer is protected in the event of a fault."

Duration of the guarantee is guaranteed for:

- Five years for immovable property (land, houses, buildings)

- Three years for moveable property (everything not considered immovable)

So, consumers are protected by not only a manufacturer's stated warrantee, but a full three years on all household appliances — not to mention all other household items! This virtually eliminates the need to purchase "extended warranties" on most items.

A Simple 240 V Lamp Conversion

One simple conversion you may be able to accomplish yourself is a basic lamp with A-type bulbs. We brought two antique lamps and converted them to 240 volts. 240 V A-type LED bulbs are readily available and can be used in your lamp; the plug can then be replaced with a 240 V plug for a compete conversion.

Beware of the Delicate Circuit Breaker Dance!

Be prepared for the first time it happens: "The dishwasher stopped. The oven, too. Lights went off. The situation had become all too clear. The flow of electricity making my dutiful appliances serve me so well had stopped."

"I went to the circuit box and quickly discovered that the problem was specifically mine. After flipping the switch and trying again, I learned that there were indeed limits to how much electric activity I could engage in simultaneously," Diana Laskaris describes in her article, *Power-Hungry in Portugal*, in a recent issue of *Portugal Living Magazine*.

"EDP, the major supplier of electricity in Portugal, gives customers an opportunity to choose their "potência contrada" or contracted power. You can select the amount based on what appliances you'll be using at one time."

"The trick is knowing what you will be using at that one time so that you don't select an amount too little or too much on a continuing basis. While it's no big deal to reset the supply switch if you trip a circuit, as I have done, it could lead to unnecessary hassles if this is something that happens often."

As I also discovered, setting your limit too low will cause annoying trips. However, it is a simple change to your electrical service contract to "upsize" your power availability, with a small monthly fee increase, of course.

I found the "small print" on the EDP website: "...*it could be associated with...the contracted power not adjusted for your consumption...Each installation has a control device that limits the power to the contracted value. When the sum of the powers of several appliances connected at the same time exceeds the contracted power, the [main] circuit breaker automatically interrupts the electrical current and the switchgear goes down."*

To be more specific, this is not an *overload* of a specific branch circuit, nor an *overload* of the main breaker. You have simply exceeded the total simultaneous electrical load allowed by your contract with the electric company. You must either (1) limit your electrical consumption by staggering the timing of your electrical appliance usage, or (2) increase the capacity by adjusting your "contracted" limit.

CHAPTER 13

BRINGING YOUR PETS

O ur fur babies are often as much a part of our family as our human family; and we wouldn't dare leave home without them. As is the case with many of our other physical possessions, some are more complicated to relocate that others.

Portugal actually has fairly liberal policies for bringing a healthy pet with you — particularly domestic dogs and cats. A special thank you goes to *Americans & FriendsPT* Facebook group for their compilation and presentation of information on this subject (as well as many others). The group's services have been invaluable to countless Americans and others relocating to Portugal. Please join their Facebook group for more information.

There will be no quarantine imposed on your pet when entering Portugal if all the requirements are met. Unless otherwise stated, the regulations below apply to domestic dogs, cats and ferrets, including service dogs. This process only covers non-commercial pets.

Professional Pet Relocation

There are actually professional pet relocation services available for those who would rather defer this process, but it is doable for the average pet owner.

There are six basic steps that must be followed to bring your pet(s) into the country:

- Preparation of Pet-Microchip & Rabies Vaccine
- Transportation Arrangements
- USDA Certificate & Notifying the PT Vet
- Travel of Pet
- Arrival in Portugal
- Local Registration

Preparation of Pet

Start a folder with all the relevant paperwork for your pet's medical history, travel arrangements, documentation, and certificates. Also, keep copies of emails and plan to carry this folder with you as you travel.

Portuguese Survival Words	
dog (*m*) cāo	(kowng)
(*f*) cadela	(ka - *de* - la)
cat gato/gata (*m/f*)	(*gaa* - too/*gaa* - ta)
bird pássaro	(*paa* - sa - roo)

The first step is to identify a USDA certified veterinarian (not just veterinary clinic) who is familiar and experiences with the regulations for providing pet certification. This process must be followed exactly.

In order to enter Portugal, your dog, cat, or ferret must be microchipped with an ISO 11784/11785 compliant 15-digit pet microchip. The corresponding chip number must also be listed on your pet's rabies certificate. The chip must be inserted prior to the vaccine as the number cannot be added to the certificate after the vaccination certificate is issued.

For pets entering Portugal from a rabies-free or rabies-controlled country (such as the US), documented proof of a current rabies vaccination that was administered (1) after the microchip was implanted, (2) no earlier than 1 year before your arrival date, and (3) at least 21 days before travel.

If this is your pet's first vaccination after microchipping, it will need to wait for at least 21 days before traveling. There is no waiting period after boosters if the previous vaccination was administered after a microchip was implanted, and the previous vaccination had not expired when the booster was given. Be prepared with appropriate documentation.

The Health Certificate must be sent to the USDA within 10 days prior to travel. Note that your vet appointment can occur up to 30 days before you travel. The USDA will return the Certificate within 72 hours prior to travel.

You must email the Portugal airport veterinarian all documentation at least 48 hours prior to travel. If flying separately, you must fly within five days of your pet.

Bubba's first Christmas in Portugal

Transportation Arrangements

When it comes to planning your pet's travel, there are several options, and many variables to consider when planning your pet's travel.

- In cabin
- As checked baggage
- Cargo
- 3rd party Pet Transport Service
- Charter flight for owners with their pets

Plan well in advance of your travel date. Before you book any flights, research all requirements by the airline. There are many different regulations, and they may change without notice!

Airlines limit the number of animals that are allowed on each flight. Weather and heat may also limit a pet's ability to board a flight. Some dog breeds are not allowed in the hold on many airlines, particularly brachycephalic (flat-faced) breeds. Check with the restrictions that your preferred airline has regarding dog breeds in the hold.

Consider the length of each flight plus the "check-in time" and what that means in terms of how long you're asking your pet to hold its bladder, etc. Many people choose to pay more and break the flights up into smaller trips to give the animal relief in this way. When you're flying with a pet, you should prioritize their comfort over the cheapest flight prices.

In Cabin

Always check the airline to find out the dimensions under the seat in front of you for the specific plane you'll be flying on.

Seat dimensions vary based on the plane and your seat assignment.

Some business and first class seats do not allow ANY pets.

You must use an airline compliant carrier. Carriers should have a waterproof bottom, an absorbent pad, secure fasteners (zippers) and ventilation on all sides. There may be more requirements – again, follow the requirements published by your airline.

Portugal Requires Documentation for Service Dogs:

Physician certification detailing the need for specific assistance:

- The ADA Privacy Act does not apply here, as this is a requirement of Portugal.
- Proof that training was done by an accredited nonprofit member organization of Assistance Dogs International
- Follow your airline's policies for flying with a service dog.

Checked Baggage

The baggage area is pressurized and climate-controlled. Thousands of people transport their pets each year using this method.

If you cannot accompany your pet, or the crate is too large or heavy to fly in the cabin, dogs and cats typically are transported as checked baggage. You must be on the SAME flight as your pet

- The combined weight of your pet and the crate must be under the airline's weight limit
- You must use an airline-compliant crate
- Check the airlines for crate dimensions and weight
- Check the airlines for prohibited breeds as checked baggage
- There are a limited number of pets per flight. Call to check
- Some airlines require a long layover between flights and will arrange for the dog to be walked (Lufthansa provides this service)
- This option may not be available year-round due to weather (specifically summer and winter). Plan accordingly and check with the airline to clarify temperature limits
- Arrive 3-4 hours early with your Pet Folder and all paperwork
- Some flights are pet-free.

Cargo

Some pets are too large for the "checked baggage" option and require special handling. These pets may need to fly cargo. Many airlines have specialists in the transportation of animals as cargo who can assist you.

- Your pet may travel on a different flight from you
- You must use an airline-compliant crate
- Contact your airline's cargo department to determine regulations
- This option may not be available year-round due to weather (specifically summer and winter)
- Pets traveling cargo are in the same pressurized and temperature-controlled holds as those in the checked baggage system.
- Confirm your space with the airline at least 24 hours prior to flight
- Follow all airline instructions for drop-off; it might not be located where you expect, so be sure to check
- The pet must be able to stand without ears touching the roof and be able to make a complete 360 degree turn
- Secure the crate with ties

3rd Party Pet Transport Service

There are many pet relocation services, including some recommended by members of *Americans & FriendsPT*. These services can be very costly. It may benefit you to also explore Charter Flights for Owners.

Charter Flight for Owners with Pet(s)

Some animals are too large for checked baggage, have special needs, or their owners want the animal to travel in the cabin with them. Contacting specialized Facebook groups such as *Chartered Air Travel With Pets* may be of assistance to those who wish to charter a flight.

USDA Pet Certificate

Once your pet is microchipped and vaccinated, you have obtained your visa, and made your flight reservations, it is time to get the USDA Health Certificate and notify the vet at your arrival airport. The timeline can become quite short, so good planning and communication are essential.

The US Department of Agriculture, Animal and Plant Health Inspection Service (APHIS) has a very helpful section of their website for pet travel from the US to Portugal.

https://www.aphis.usda.gov/aphis/pet-travel/by-country/eu/pettravel-portugal

To bring your pet(s) to Portugal, you will need a certificate for non-commercial transportation. This certificate allows you, or a designated person, traveling within five days before or after your pet(s), to bring up to five pets into the country.

You must submit the EU Health Certificate for USDA approval no sooner than 10 days before you arrive in Portugal.

Once the vet has completely filled in the document, and you have reviewed the certificate to make sure everything is accurate, you will need to submit this document to USDA for endorsement. You have a few options to submit:

1. Use the Veterinary Export Health Certification System (VEHCS). Be sure your vet supports this method as it is the fastest, most reliable method.

2. Alternatively, you may ship the paperwork to the USDA Endorsement Office serving your state, although this will take additional valuable time to complete the process.

NOTE: For both options, you will need to purchase an overnight return shipping label with Saturday delivery. Ensure that you are using an address that can receive overnight mail just prior to your departure.

See the USDA website for other options.

Notifying the Portuguese Airport Vet

Remember you must notify the airport veterinarian office of your arrival details and provide attachments of all the relevant paperwork you got from your veterinarian at least 48 hours before your arrival (Portugal time!)

Email the following documents to the airport veterinarian at your arriving city:

- The Pet Arrival Notification Form (an example is in the Appendix)
  - Name of owner
  - Airline, flight number, and time of arrival
  - Address in Portugal after arrival
  - Email address

- Contact telephone number
- Pet breed
- Certificate from USDA
- Rabies certificate (must include microchip number)
- Microchip certificate (must show date inserted)

Bring a copy of the email and a hardcopy of all documents in the pet folder in your carry-on luggage, and be prepared to show them everything.

Have 40€ per animal available upon arrival for the veterinarian exam and taxes. Whether you can pay with a credit card may depend on the airport and may change over time. If you want to be 100% safe, be prepared to pay with cash.

For Pets Traveling Cargo

You will need to send an email with the above information as well as the intended date and time of appointment for pickup of documentation and cargo claim, to the Cargo Claim office <u>Subject Line: Importation of Live Pets into Portugal</u>.

It is critical to receive a response from Cargo Claim. If you do not receive a response within 24 hours, email them again to confirm the appointment time.

Travel With Your Pet

If a pet is traveling in the cabin with its owner, TSA must screen it at the security checkpoint. Below is what pet owners can expect: (subject to change)

- All pets should be brought to the security checkpoint in a hand-held travel carrier. Remove the pet from the carrier just prior to the beginning of the screening process.

- Do not put the pet into the X-ray tunnel, which is used to screen a passenger's personal property and carry-on luggage. Place the empty travel carrier on the belt to be X-rayed.

- You should maintain control of your pet with a leash and remember to remove the leash when carrying your pet through the metal detector. Animal carriers will undergo a visual and/or physical inspection.

- A TSA officer may give the pet owner's hands an explosive trace detection swab to ensure there is no explosive residue on the hands.

- Once the screening process is completed, owners should return the pet to the travel carrier at the re-composure area, away from the security checkpoint for the safety of the pet as well as other passengers.

- You may request a private room screening if you are afraid that your pet may get loose when holding in the screening area.

Arrival in Portugal

Accompanied pets entering Portugal by air from non-EU countries must do so at Border Inspection Posts at international airports in Lisbon, Oporto, Funchal, Ponta Delgada, Terceira Island or Faro. Unaccompanied pets must enter at Lisbon, Oporto or Faro. The process is dependent on whether the pet traveled in cabin, as checked baggage, or as cargo.

Pets that Traveled In Cabin

Since these pets were traveling with you, you can proceed directly to the airport veterinarian office and present your documents as stated above. The veterinarian will provide you with a receipt and proof of examination. Be prepared to show this document to the customs officer prior to exiting the airport. Follow airport specific information shown below.

Pets that Traveled as Checked Baggage

These pets will have traveled on the same plane and will be brought to the baggage claim area where they can be retrieved prior to going to the airport veterinarian.

Pets that Traveled as Cargo

Upon arrival at your destination, you must go to the cargo area office and claim the shipping documentation for your pet(s). This is usually away from the main airport terminal. Once you receive the documentation, you must get the veterinarian clearance.

Lisbon (LIS) Airport

The email address for the veterinarian's office in Lisbon is: pcflisboaa@dgav.pt. Use this address to email all documents

Porto (OPO) Airport

The email address for the veterinarian's office in Porto is: pcfportoa@dgav.pt

Faro (FAO) Airport

The email address for the veterinarian's office in Faro is: pets.entrypoint.fao@dgav.pt

Local Registration

The veterinarian clearance form is good for four months of travel within the EU if the rabies vaccination documented on it does not expire. Hence, you should visit a local veterinarian upon your arrival to Portugal to examine your pet and register with the local jurisdiction. Portugal also has different vaccine requirements than the US, so your pet may require additional vaccination(s).

> *We found a veterinarian who comes to our home, provides all necessary services, and for a reasonable cost - she is wonderful!*

The European Union has a system for relocating pets that uses a personalized pet passport. This EU Pet Passport contains the animal's 15-digit chip code as well as all vaccine information. It is required when traveling on metros, buses, trains, and between EU countries, so be sure to ask your veterinarian about this passport if you intend to transport your pet within the EU.

Please practice due diligence, and research all applicable information regarding pet relocation and transport, especially regarding pets other than dogs and cats.

Portuguese Survival Phrases

Is it safe?	É seguro?	(e se - *goo* - roo)
I'm lost		Estou perdido/perdida (*m/f*)
		(shtoh per - *dee* - doo/per - *dee* - da)

CHAPTER 14

HOUSEHOLD GOODS

By the time you have decided to make the big move, you will probably have a pretty good idea what, if any, household goods you intend to bring with you. You will likely have decided to forgo bringing your car, large pieces of furniture, electrical tools and appliances, and most of your personal items that can be easily replaced in your new homeland.

Truly, most household items can be replaced for about what it would cost you to have them shipped to Europe — and that would be replacing them with all new furniture and appliances!

Portugal has many furniture retailers with a vast selection of styles and price points. IKEA has multiple outlets and offers home delivery. They also offer Task Rabbit assembly services for those of us intimidated by the words "requires some assembly." Check out IKEA.pt to shop online.

We were actually able to purchase many pieces of household furniture from IKEA and have them delivered and assembled prior to our arrival. Our real estate agent helped coordinate this effort for us.

There are also numerous retail outlets which carry other household goods and appliances, many of which are well recognized European manufacturers.

In addition al local Portuguese retailers, amazon.es (Spain) provides a vast array of household products, most with one to three day home delivery to Portugal addresses. Bear in mind that purchases within the EU are not subject to import taxes, however purchases made outside the EU (such as US and UK) are subject to rather hefty import taxes.

Do your research, look at multiple options, and be open minded about purchasing products from unfamiliar manufacturers, retailers, online sources, and other countries. Virtually everything you need and want will be available to you in your new home.

Portuguese Survival Words		
Yes	Sim	(seeng)
No	Não	(nowng)
Sorry	Desculpe	(desh - *kool* - pe)
Please	For favor	(poor fa - *vor*)
Hello	Olá	(o - *laa*)

CHAPTER 15

HEALTHCARE OPTIONS

S everal healthcare options are available once you reside in Portugal. Low premiums and copayments, and first class healthcare make it one of the most attractive benefits of living here. Most immigrants, especially retirees will take advantage of one or both of the following healthcare systems:

The first is the National Health Services, or SNS as it's known in Portuguese. All expats are eligible for care. All residents in Portugal qualify to use the public healthcare system. Once you have obtained your residence card from SEF (Servico de Entrangeiros e Fronteiras), your SNS number (Utente de Saude) can be fully activated, allowing you full access to the services of the national healthcare system. Your SEF appointment finalizing your immigration status is usually about 90 days following your arrival into the country.

The other option is voluntary private healthcare. While not as popular as it is in other countries, private healthcare still plays an important role in Portuguese society. There are a number of national health insurance providers as well as international companies that serve the expat community. (Names you might hear include Multicare, Mudum, Allianz, AdvanceCare, CUF, and Medis.)

For the uninsured, or for those who wish to access the private healthcare system without buying insurance, basic healthcare costs in Portugal are reasonable. The cost of seeing a general practitioner is usually around 60€. An initial visit to a specialist is around 100€. Basic dental cleaning starts at about 25€.

It is not uncommon for expats to utilize a combination of these different healthcare systems. For instance, all HIV prevention (PrEP) and treatment is covered under the National Health Services. Routine medical care however may be more quickly received by using the private healthcare system and private insurance, as appointments and referrals may take longer in the National Heath Service. And, in some instances, it may be advantageous to pay out of pocket for some medical and dental services, and medications.

If you arrive to Portugal with prescription medications for chronic conditions, you may be able to have those refilled at local pharmacies by presenting your US prescription. So, bring your original prescription labels, even of you repackage your medications for travel. Some medications may be refilled without a new prescription, although of course, Controlled Substances probably will not be refilled without a new prescription.

Portugal National EMERGENCY Number

112

In an emergency during normal business hours, American citizens should contact the Embassy at +351 21-77-2122

CHAPTER 16

BANKING IN PORTUGAL

Establishing a bank account in Portugal is one of the first steps you need to take when preparing to apply for a residence visa. A fiscal number is a tax identification number issued in Portugal to anyone who wishes to undertake any official matters in Portugal. It is known as a *Número de Identificação Fiscal* (NIF) and is sometimes referred to as a *Número de Contribuinte*. It is required for nearly every official process in Portugal — from opening a bank account, to setting up an account with a utility company, to buying a property.

Both applying for a NIF, and opening a bank account may be accomplished with or without the assistance of a personal representative such as an attorney. This process is obviously simpler for you with a help of an attorney, especially if you are doing this from the US.

Most large banks in Portugal welcome new customer from the US, however, some are now not allowing nonresidents to open new accounts.

According to golden-visa-portugal.info, Portuguese banks are highly advanced. Their system is extremely developed.

All banks in the country are linked to its Multibanco system. Portugal is a Eurozone country, so that you can transfer money from any other Eurozone country without any conversion fees.

If you need to make any direct payments or transfers, you can easily do so with a Portuguese bank account. You will also receive a debit card, and credit card if necessary. Additionally, you can use checks, and you have the option of choosing if you want overdraft protection or not for your account.

Golden Visa Portugal ranks these five Portugal banks as the best banks for foreigners:

- Millennium BCP
- Caixa Geral de Depósitos
- Novobanco
- Banco BPI
- ActivoBank

Yes, Your Social Security can be Deposited Directly

You can use Form SSA-1199-PE, Direct Deposit Sign-Up Form (Portugal), to arrange for direct deposit of your Social Security monthly benefits into your Portuguese bank. Form SSA-1199-SE is included in the Appendix at the end of this book.

Warning: Be sure to maintain your current address and contact information with the Social Security Administration. They send verification request forms annually to non-resident citizens, mailed to your physical address on file. If you fail to respond within 90 days, they send a reminder notice. If you still do not respond, they *SUSPEND* your Social Security benefit!

So, if your address is not current, you don't realize they've mailed you a form; so they mail a reminder notice, which you are also not aware of. Then one day, when you least expect it — NO Social Security payment! Chaos is guaranteed to ensue. You will call Social Security Administration, wait on 'eternal hold' until you are connected to a live human, update your address and contact information, complete the necessary form, deliver it to the Social Security Administration office at the US Embassy — then WAIT for your account to be reinstated, and your missed payment to appear. Not fun!

What About my US Bank Account(s)?

Needless to say, your Portuguese bank accounts will be in Euros (€) and your US bank accounts are in US Dollars ($). There are several reasons you wish to maintain a US bank account while in Portugal. You may have US-based services that must be paid in dollars, and you may order goods and services from US-based companies, for use in the US (such as gifts for friends and family located in the US). You may also retain streaming services and other services that you

---

Portuguese Tip
Tips on meals are appreciated but there is no overall tipping culture in Portugal (tourist zones are an exception). One or two euros—or about 5% of the meal's cost—is the norm. Pocket change returned when paying for beverages is enough.

---

will continue to use in Portugal, that require payment in US dollars.

Also, if you have a student loan account, or an IRS account that is connected to your bank account, it may need to remain active while you're abroad.

CHAPTER 17

TAX CONSIDERATIONS

Advantages of Non-Habitual Residency

Obtaining Non-Habitual Residence (NHR) in Portugal comes with key advantages that can make your choice a little bit easier. Check out the key advantages of the NHR tax regime below:

- For ten years, the taxation on income obtained from a Portuguese source is at a fixed rate of 20% (personal income tax), if derived from a high-value-added activity

- For pension incomes, including Social Security retirement income, or employment and self-employment income obtained abroad, there is no double taxation

- The possibility to pass on wealth or estate without inheritance or gift taxes

What is Meant by the Term 'Non-Habitual'?

Non-habitual does not imply that you need to be a tax resident of another country besides Portugal. It simply refers to the fact that the tax regime of NHR is valid for a limited time of ten years.

How do You Become a Non-Habitual Resident in Portugal?

- You must not have been a resident in Portugal for the previous five years

- You must register at the local tax office as a tax resident in Portugal

- Request enrollment as a Non Habitual Resident electronically

- There is no requirement for a minimum-stay duration

- The NHR status may be granted for ten years, and the application for NHR must be filed with the Portuguese tax authorities before the 31st of March the year after settling in Portugal

---

FBAR Form
Foreign Bank and Financial Accounts Report
Financial Crimes Enforcement Network (FinCEN) Form 114

A U.S. person, including a citizen, resident, corporation, partnership, limited liability company, trust and estate, must file an FBAR to report (1) a financial interest in or signature or other authority over at least one financial account located outside the United States, (2) if the aggregate value of those foreign financial accounts exceeded $10,000 at any time during the calendar year reported.

The report may be filed online via The BSA E-Filing System, and must be filed annually by April 15 following the calendar year being reported.

CHAPTER 18

MEDICARE OPTIONS

Medicare benefits.

After age 65, US residents should be enrolled in Medicare, the federal healthcare plan for seniors. Medicare consists of several components, offering healthcare coverage for various aspects of your healthcare. Most seniors are enrolled in multiple parts. Most of these benefits do *not* provide coverage while you are outside the United States.

Part A - Hospital Insurance: Cost $0 for most people; Deductible $1,600 for each hospital admission, per benefit period

Helps cover inpatient care in hospitals, skilled nursing facility care, hospice care, and home health care.

Part B - Medical Insurance: Cost $164.90 each month; Annual Deductible $226; 20% co-payment
Helps cover services from doctors and other health care providers

- Outpatient care
- Home health care
- Durable medical equipment (like wheelchairs, walkers, hospital beds, and other equipment)
- Many preventive services (like screenings, shots or vaccines, and yearly "wellness" visits

Late enrollment penalty - You'll pay an extra 10% for each year you could have signed up for Part B, but didn't. According to AARP, if you live outside the US and are not entitled to premium-free Part A benefits, you cannot enroll in Part A or Part B. Instead, you get a special enrollment period to sign up that begins during the month you return as a US resident, and extends for up to two months afterward. If you enroll at that time, you are not liable for Part A or Part B late penalties.

Part D - Drug coverage: Helps cover the cost of prescription drugs (including many recommended shots or vaccines)

Late enrollment penalty - A surcharge is permanently added to the monthly premium of your Part D prescription drug plan if you fail to sign up when you're first eligible for Medicare, and you don't have similar drug coverage. If you've been living outside the US, you can avoid late penalties if you sign up with a Part D plan within two months of your return.

Medicare Supplemental Insurance (Medi-Gap): Extra insurance that you can buy from a private company that helps pay your share of costs in original Medicare. Policies are standardized, and in most states named by letters, like Plan G or Plan K.

Part C - Medicare Advantage: If you are eligible for Medicare, you have a choice to receive your benefits through original Medicare or a Medicare Advantage plan. Medicare Advantage is a Medicare-approved plan from a private company that offers an alternative to original Medicare for your health and drug coverage. These "bundled" plans include Part A, Part B, and usually Part D benefits.

Living Abroad - Medicare offers minimal, if any, benefits, and only for a short period of time, to non-resident citizens.

If you're eligible for Medicare, and neither you nor your spouse is working, you usually can enroll in Medicare while living outside the U.S. But you have a decision to make:

Either pay monthly Medicare Part B premiums for coverage you can't use outside the United States, or delay enrollment until you return to the U.S.

Both Medicare supplement insurance, commonly called Medi-gap, and Medicare Advantage, also known as Part C, are tied to enrolling in Part B and living in the United States.

Your decision may hinge on whether you plan to live out of the country for a short period or long term. If you plan to be an expatriate permanently, you won't need to worry about signing up and potential late enrollment penalties.

Medicaid is a joint federal and state program that helps cover medical costs for some people with limited income and resources. Medicaid offers benefits not normally covered by Medicare, like nursing home care and personal care services. Eligibility for Medicaid is different in each state with varying rules for your income and resources, and being a resident of the state.

Your Medical Record. Please — for your own sake, and your future medical providers — bring a thorough record of your personal medical history, including allergies, chronic conditions, surgeries, and medications. If you have imaging (X-ray, CAT, MRI) reports, bring copies of these. Even though they will be in English, and your new providers will likely be Portuguese speakers, most doctors here also speak functional English, and will be able to read your medical reports. A sample Medical History form is included in the Appendix at the end of this book.

CHAPTER 19

FINAL THOUGHTS

Explore Portugal Before you Decide. One might assume this "goes without saying," however you also know what they say when we "assume..." Plan ahead, take an exploratory trip (or two) to the country; see a few areas, and spend some time in the neighborhoods. See if this is really the place where you want to live. And what do you like to do in your spare time? Hang out at the beach, in the city? Would you prefer to be more secluded? In a rural area? Portugal has all this to offer; you just need to spend some time exploring and discover an area that suits you.

Day of Travel Tips. The big day has arrived; are you really ready? One can never be completely certain! But careful planning and preparation is your best defense against a last minute meltdown.

- Use a checklist. Yours will be different than ours. Develop your checklist based on the recommendations found here in the D7 Checklist, and the Timeline, as well as your own personal needs.

- Bring a "Day of Travel" folder. In addition to your Passports, which should be carried on your person, carry a folder with paper copies of anything and everything you may need that day:

- Flight Reservations
- Boarding Passes - Yes, even if you have them on your cellphone. Save these for your SEF appointment. (*I left the secure area at one point, and was not allowed to re-enter without a paper boarding pass - because it was an international flight. I was required to go to a nearby business center, email my boarding pass to them, and have it* <u>*printed on paper*</u> *before I could re-enter!*)
- Luggage Claim Tickets. Save these for your SEF appointment
- Travel and Medical Insurance documents. Save these for your SEF appointment
- Pet travel documentation
- Personal medical histories with Medication Lists
- Local Transportation Reservations (names and phone numbers)
- Accommodation Reservations (hotel, apartment addresses and phone numbers)

- Consider arriving at your departure city the day *before* your flight. I can't think of anything much worse than missing a flight connection, your luggage not being loaded onto your intercontinental flight, or missing your flight due to a delayed or cancelled connecting flight. Here is how we accomplished our big day:

We moved from Palm Springs, California to Lisbon, flying from San Francisco (SFO) directly to Lisbon (LIS). My husband and I were traveling with 11 bags and our beloved "deer chihuahua," Bubba.

We drove from Palm Springs to San Francisco in a rented minivan the day before our flight. We actually had packed the van with all our bags, and were waiting for FedEx to deliver our USDA pet certificate so we could begin our journey that day! Once we had received the certificate, we drove to San Francisco and stayed at a hotel near the airport. We returned the van to the rental agency, had some dinner, and got a good night's rest.

Then, the morning of the big day, the hotel shuttle delivered us, with our 11 bags and Bubba to SFO to board our TAP Airlines Flight to Lisbon - with time to spare! When we checked in at the counter, the first thing the agent asked for was Bubba's documentation. She immediately inspected each page, running her fingers over the embossed seals to verify their authenticity. (Good thing we had waited for the original documents to be delivered, rather than present the copies without the embossed seals!)

Once in the aircraft, we were delighted to find that we had an entire row to ourselves! The three of us enjoyed a delightful flight to our new European home!

Living in a New Culture. Make every day an adventure, get to know your neighborhood and your neighbors. Be prepared for entirely new experiences. You will immediately notice differences in the streets, sidewalks, and buildings. You will likely also notice graffiti — a lot of it! Don't worry, it doesn't necessarily represent the same image of gangs, lawlessness and crime that you have probably learned to associate with graffiti from other places. Some of it is actually quite artistic and beautiful.

You will find narrower streets and sidewalks, mostly cobblestone, which can be uneven and sometimes slippery to walk on! Be careful when it rains! In general, however, you will find a very "first-world" country, with hundreds of years of history and a very well-developed infrastructure: highways; electrical, telephone, cellular, and internet systems; and water and sewage systems are all highly functional. As part of the European Union, health and safety standards are also comparable to other EU countries.

Pre-Arrival Preparations. There are a few things you can arrange for prior to your arrival. You should pre-arrange having your home cleaned as it is not customary for the landlord to have your apartment cleaned for you — really! You may be able to have furniture and appliances delivered and set up, and also have your utility services connected and activated.

There are companies which specifically provide that service for those of us moving in from out of the area. One such company that we used is Liveasylisbon.com. For a flat rate, they had our gas, electric, and water accounts activated, as well as cable TV, internet, and cellphone service. Our cellular SIM cards were there waiting for us when we arrived. And the furniture had been assembled by TaskRabbit. So we had a bed to sleep on the first night.

An excellent resource for navigating the connection of your home utilities is found at https://www.beportugal.com/utilities-in-portugal/.

Mail and Delivery Services. Portugal CTT (Correios de Portugal) is Portugal's national postal service provider, delivering registered or express mails and parcels across Portugal and internationally. CTT operates as both the national postal service of Portugal and a commercial group

 with subsidiaries operating in banking, e-commerce, and other postal services. International mail between the US and Portugal is readily available. Keep in mind that transit time will probably be longer than you expect, sometimes several weeks.

Several other local and international delivery services are available, including UPS, DHL, and FedEx. Household goods are commonly purchased through amazon.es (Spain) and delivered by various companies with excellent efficiency. One significant difference is that most deliveries other than regular mail require receipt by a person at the point of delivery; don't count on them leaving your package on your doorstep here!

Addresses in Portugal. Addresses in Portugal are a very different format than we are accustomed to in the US. Here's a primer on street addresses:

Example:

> Sr. Ricardo Lopes
> Rua Maria Garcia 10 - 2 Esq
> 1800-123 Lisboa Portugal

First Line - Title, Full Name
Second Line - Street Name, Door number - Floor, Unit
Third Line - Postal Code, City, Country

Note that the street address lists the street first, then the "door number" (rather than a building number, which are numbered sequentially, with odd and even numbers on opposite sides of the street); followed by the floor number; then unit location on the floor. The floor number refers to the floor within the building, with ground floor being "RC," and "1" being the first floor *above* the ground floor! "Cv" (Cave) refers to a floor below ground level.

The individual apartment designation refers to the location of the apartment door at the stair landing - which may or *may not* correspond to that side of the building when facing it from the street! "Esq" (esquerda) refers to the Left, and "Drt" (direita) refers to Right. You may occasionally see "Frt" for Front, in the case of three apartment doors on a floor.

Mail Forwarding. To help manage your mail, you may want to consider having your US mail forwarded to a family member, friend, or a professional mail forwarding service. Several professional services are available which provide efficient handling of your US mail while you are abroad. They can scan and email your mail to you, and you can designate which actions to take on your behalf. You may only need this type of service for six months or so, and the costs are reasonable.

Keep in mind, however, that you may need to keep a physical address (other than a mail forwarding address) for other reasons. US banks will often require a physical address.

Voting from Abroad. US citizens living outside the US are eligible to vote in US elections as overseas voters! You must meet the same eligibility requirements as other US voters, such as being 18 years old by the general election, but it doesn't matter how long you have been outside the US or if you were registered to vote before you left.

All overseas voters are eligible to vote in federal elections, that is, for President, US Senator, and US House of Representatives.

An excellent resource for complete information on voting from abroad can be found at www.votefromabroad.org.

Import Taxes in the EU. While products are readily available from countries throughout Europe, be aware that you will be assessed import taxes for anything arriving from outside the EU. So ordering from amazon.es (Spain), for instance, is tax-free; however ordering from the UK will incur taxes. So, you want to advise your friends and family in the States *not* to send things to you. Besides the cost of international mail or transportation, *you* will be assessed import tax on those items. And sometimes they can be a hefty tax.

Virtual Private Network (VPN) is a service that helps you stay private online. A VPN establishes a secure, encrypted connection between your computer and the internet, providing a private tunnel for your data and communications. Ultimately, a VPN is a important and valuable tool. It completely secures your private and personal information and prevents your data from getting into the hands of third parties who can use this information against you. For such reasons, it's recommended to keep your VPN on for most, if not all, of the time. A VPN may allow you to access streaming content and websites that may otherwise be restricted in your area. For instance, your hometown local news channel may restrict access from Europe; however, you may find that using a VPN will allow you to keep up on your hometown news. It may also be useful to maintain access to a US-based bank account.

Telecommunication Services. One of the most common questions I have been asked is how to stay in contact with friends and family after you move to Portugal. Of course e-mail works anywhere you have internet access, and there are various telecommunication and mobile-based platforms to help you stay in touch. Cellular service is readily available in Portugal, providing voice calling and SMS (text messaging) services throughout the country.

Messenger. Facebook's Messenger services allow text messaging as well as audio and video calling over the internet, provided both parties are subscribed to Messenger.

Google Voice. Another useful tool is Google Voice. Google Voice is a telephone service that provides a US phone number to Google customers in the US, and Google Workspace customers in Canada, Denmark, France, the

Netherlands, Portugal, Spain, Sweden, Switzerland and the United Kingdom. You may also "port" your existing US telephone/cell number to Google Voice and continue to use it. Voice allows you to call all US numbers and allows you to receive calls from all US numbers without the other party subscribing to the platform. There may also be other similar platforms available. Be sure to set up your phone service *before* you leave the US. You will be required to verify yourself with a US telephone/cellphone number.

WhatsApp. WhatsApp is an internationally available freeware, cross-platform, centralized instant messaging and voice-over-IP service owned by US tech conglomerate Meta. It allows users to send text and voice messages, make voice and video calls, and share images, documents, user locations, and other content. WhatsApp is commonly used throughout Europe for texting and phone calls. It is available for your mobile device as well as your computer. It is free, very efficient, and available worldwide. Groups can also be set up to send/receive messages to multiple users concurrently; a very useful feature for groups of family or friends! Users must subscribe to access this platform.

Integrate into Your New Home. For some of us (introverts) meeting new people and joining new groups isn't as easy as it is for others. Fortunately, there are lots of people relocating to various parts of the world, and there are plenty of resources to help integrate! Since we moved here, we have joined a Facebook local expats social group, a Face book LGBTQ+ happy hour group, a community choir, a men's yoga group, and a MeetUp dinner group. Each group has locals and expats from multiple countries that are all looking to make acquaintances and friends. Some groups will be a "better fit" than others, but there are plenty of them — just put yourself out there.

Learn the Language. We also found multiple language classes available for learners at all levels. There are also tutors available for online and face-to-face instruction. It may be a challenge to learn a new language, but it's worth the effort. The locals appreciate that we try to speak their language, and are usually helpful in correcting our mistakes!

Local Customs and Holidays. There are plenty of local customs and a multitude of holidays in Portugal. For starters, many stores, shops, and restaurants are closed daily for two to three hours. (think "siesta) The Portuguese have found a key to relieving stress, building solid family ties, and ensuring that they get enough sleep. This key is the siesta. That is right, much in Portugal shuts down between the hours of noon and three, as people return home to eat, sleep, and spend time with their families. Entire cities may be rendered virtual ghost towns during these hours and the streets may be empty as shops' doors are closed and the lights are off. The tourist areas are less likely to strictly observe these routine interruptions in local tourism.

There are also plenty of federal and local holidays which can close down businesses and services throughout the communities. A cursory look at the local "2023 Lisbon Holidays" calendar shows at least 15 Portuguese holidays which likely include widespread "interruptions" in local services. In addition there's another 20 "Lisbon Event Days." The Portuguese people like to party!

Lisbon "Well Prepared" for an Eventual Earthquake

ThePortugalNews.com reports that the Mayor of Lisbon, Carlos Moedas, who is also a civil engineer, has announced that the city has excellent preparation for seismic risk and response to catastrophes.

"In relation to earthquakes, my statement has to do with the excellent preparation of our civil protection team, the excellent preparation of our firefighters and the excellent preparation of our engineers."

Moedas said that the capital is "extremely prepared" for the possibility of an earthquake similar to the one that happened in Turkey and Syria, including a tsunami warning system.

Useful Mobile Apps

In addition to the communication apps, here is a list of my most used mobile apps for getting by every day:

Google Translate is a multilingual neural machine translation service developed by Google to translate text, documents and websites from one language into another. It offers a website interface, and a mobile app for Android and iOS. One of its most useful features is the ability to take an in-app photo, and the app will translate immediately a sign or menu, for instance.

Apple Maps and **Google Maps** are both extremely useful; sometimes one provides better search results than the other. I often search both, and take the results that better suit my immediate situation. Be sure to enter your "Home" location and other frequently used locations as favorites, so you can recall them quickly and easily.

Uber and **Bolt** both provide rideshare services in Portugal. As when using the map apps, these apps will  likely provide you with different results. I usually try both apps, compare prices and wait times, then decide which service to use. Again, be sure to enter your your "Home" and other frequently used locations as favorites, so they can recalled quickly and easily. And don't forget to enter your billing information so they are ready to use when you are!

In addition to rideshare services, both Uber and Bolt have electric bicycles and scooters available in some areas. Some areas also have scooters available from other vendors, such as Whoosh, Bird, Superpedestrian/Link, and Lime. Each has their own mobile app, which requires pre-registration and billing information to use. I recommend having at lease two or three scooter apps if you intend to ride rentable bikes or scooters.

CP (Comboios de Portugal) is a free app for train service in Portugal, with the following functions: search and purchase, next trains, your tickets, your activity, your timetables, discounts and benefits, alerts, and information.

TTSL (Transtejo & Soflusa) is a public ferry company operating between Lisbon, on the right bank of the Tagus

River, to the left bank of the river at Trafaria, Porto Brandão, Cacilhas, Seixal, Barreiro and Montijo. If you use their services, this app is useful to monitor ferry schedules and and planned interruptions in service.

TAP Air Portugal also has a very useful mobile app, which allows purchases, upgrades, ticketing, check-in, flight status, and notifications via your cellphone.

MB Way In addition to you local bank app, MB Way

(Multibanco) has a very useful mobile app, which can be used for point of sale and online purchases, transferring funds to and from other people for services, and withdrawals from local ATMs.

CHAPTER 20

APPENDIX

D7 VISA APPLICATION CHECKLIST

D7 VISA APPLICATION

LUGGAGE CERTIFICATE

PORTUGAL CRIMINAL BACKGROUND CHECK

PET ARRIVAL

SOCIAL SECURITY SSA-1199-SE FORM

PERSONAL MEDICAL HISTORY

D7 Application Checklist

- [ ] Completed Application for National Visa

- [ ] Original or Certified Copy of Passport

- [ ] Proof of Travel and Medical Insurance

- [ ] FBI Background Check Report

- [ ] Copies of US and Portuguese Bank Statements (3 months)

- [ ] Passive Income Documentation

- [ ] Proof of Accommodation

- [ ] Money Order for Visa Fees

- [ ] Passport Photograph

- [ ] Reservation of Outbound Flight

- [ ] Portugal Criminal Background Check Form

- [ ] Lawyer Letter of Recommendation

- [ ] Documentation of Fiscal Identification Number (NIF)

- [ ] Personal Statement Letter

- [ ] Release of Liability for Passport Mailing

PORTUGAL

S. R.

Application for national visa (residence and temporary stay)

This application is free

	FOTO

1. Surname (Family name) (x)		**FOR OFFICIAL USE ONLY**
2. Surname at birth (Former family name (s)) (x)		Date of application:
3. First name (s) (Given name(s)) (x)		Visa application number:
4. Date of birth (day-month-year)	5. Place of birth / 6. Country of birth	7. Current nationality / Nationality of birth, if different	**Application lodged at:** □ Embassy/Consulate
8. Sex □ Male □ Female	9. Marital status □ Single □ Married □ Separated □ Divorced □ Widow(er) □ Other (please specify)	**Name:** □ Other
10. In the case of minors Surname , first name, address (if different from applicant's) and nationality of parental authority □ Father □ Mother		File handled by: **Supporting documents:** □ Travel document □ Means of subsistence
Surname, first name, address (if different from applicant's) and nationality of legal guardian		□ Invitation □ Means of transport
11. National identity number, where applicable		□ TMI □ Others:
12. Type of travel document: □ Ordinary passport □ Other travel document (please specify)		**Visa decision:** □ Refused □ Issued: □ E □ D
13. Number of the travel document	14. Date of issue / 15. Valid until / 16. Issued by	**Valid:** From Until
17. Applicant's home address and e-mail adress	Telephone number	**Number of entries** □ 2 □ Multiple
18. Residence in a country other than the country of current nationality □ No □ Yes. Residence permit or equivalent .... N.° .... Valid until		**Number of days:**
19. Current occupation		

Page 143

20. Employer and employer's address and telephone number. For students, name and address of educational establishment.	
21. Main purpose (s) of the journey: □ Professional internship □ Family reunion □ Volunteering □ Sports □ Accompany a family member submitted to medical treatment □ Medical treatment □ Study □ Others (please specify)	
22. Member Sate of destination PORTUGAL	23. Member Sate of first entry
24. Number of entries request □ two entries (residence) □ multiple entries (temporary stay)	25. Duration of the intended stays Indicate the number of days

(x) Fields 1-3 shall be filled in in accordance with the data in the travel document.

26. Visas issued during the past three years □ No □ Yes. Valid from .... to	
27. e 28. NOT APLICABLE	
29. Intended date of arrival in the Schengen area	30. Intended date of departure from the Schengen area
31. Surname and first name of the inviting person(s) in Portugal or, if not applicable, name of hotel (s) or temporary accommodation(s) in Portugal.	
Address and e-mail address of inviting person(s) / hotel(s)/ temporary accommodation(s)	Telephone and telefax
32. Name and address of inviting company/ organization	Telephone and telefax of company/ organization
Surname and first name, address, telephone, telefax and e-mail address of contact person in company/organization	
33. Cost of travelling and living during the applicant's stay is covered	

□ by the applicant himself/herself	□ by a sponsor (host, company, organization), please specify
	    □ referred to in field 31 or 32
	    □ others (please specify):

Means of support □ Cash □ Traveller's cheques □ Credit card □ Prepaid accommodation □ Prepaid transport □ Other (please specify:	Means of support □ Cash □ Accommodation provided □ All expenses covered during the stay □ Prepaid transport □ Other (please specify):
34. NOT APLICABLE	35.NOT APLICABLE
36. Place and date	37.Signature (for minors, signature of parental authority/ legal guardian)

Page 144

I am aware that the visa fee is not refunded if the visa is refused.

I am aware of the need to have an adequate travel medical insurance that will be able to assume medical expenses, including urgent medical care and possible repatriation.

I am aware of and consent to the following: the collection of the data required by this application form and the taking of my photograph and, if applicable, the taking of fingerprints, are mandatory for the examination of the visa application; and any personal data concerning me which appear on the visa application form, as well as my fingerprints and my photograph will be supplied to the relevant authorities of the Member States and processed by those authorities, for the purposes of a decision on my visa application.

Such data as well as data concerning the decision taken on my application or a decision whether to annul, revoke or extend a visa issued will be entered into, and stored in the Rede de Pedidos de Visto (RPV), which it will be accessible to the visa authorities and the authorities competent for carrying out checks on visas at external borders and also to the immigration and asylum authorities in the Member States for the purposes of verifying whether the conditions for the legal entry into, stay and residence on the territory of the Member States are fulfilled, of identifying persons who do not or who no longer fulfil these conditions, of examining an asylum application and of determining responsibility for such examination. Such data will be also accessible to the competent authorities for the examination and decision on the applications for residence permits or to extend a visa issued. The authority of the Member State responsible for processing the data is: Direção Geral dos Assuntos Consulares e Comunidades Portuguesas (DGACCP).

I am aware that I have the right to obtain notification of the data relating to me, and of the Member State which transmitted the data, and to request that data relating to me which are inaccurate be corrected and that data relating to me processed unlawfully be deleted. At my express request, the authority examining my application will inform me of the manner in which I may exercise my right to check the personal data concerning me and have them corrected or deleted, including the related remedies according to the national law of the State concerned. The national supervisory authority of that Member State [Comissão Nacional de Proteção de Dados (CNPD) - Rua de São Bento nº. 148 – 3º, 1200-821 Lisboa, www.cnpd.pt] will hear claims concerning the protection of personal data.

I declare that to the best of my knowledge all particulars supplied by me are correct and complete. I am aware that any false statements will lead to my application being rejected or to the annulment of a visa already granted and may also render me liable to prosecution under the Portuguese law.

I undertake to leave Portugal before the expiry of the visa, if granted. I have been informed that possession of a visa is only one of the prerequisites for entry into Portugal. The mere fact that a visa has been granted to me does not mean that I will be entitled to compensation if I fail to comply with the national legislation applicable - Law n.º 23/07 de 4/07 amended by the Law n.º 29/12 de 9/08 and I am therefore refused entry. The prerequisites for entry will be checked again on entry into the Portuguese territory.

Place and date	Signature (for minors, signature of parental authority/ legal guardian)

SAMPLE LUGGAGE CERTIFICATE

EXAMPLE OF DECLARATION

Declaração

Eu, _____, portador do passaporte nº _____, emitido em _____, aos __/__/____, para os devidos efeitos declaro por minha honra que os artigos abaixo mencionados fazem parte do recheio da minha residência há mais de __ (meses/anos), sita em _____ (morada), onde tenho residência principal há mais de doze meses consecutivos, que estão pagos na totalidade e que irei transferir a minha residência principal para Portugal, para a morada _____, no prazo de __ (meses/dias).

San Francisco, __/__/____

[Assinatura]

> *ENGLISH (for reference only; must be submitted in Portuguese)*
>
> Declaration
>
> I, _____, bearer of passport No. _____, issued in _____, at __/__/____, for the due purposes, declare on my honor that the items mentioned below have been part of the contents of my residence for more than __ (months/years) , located at _____ (address), where I have had my main residence for more than twelve consecutive months, which are paid in full and that I will transfer my main residence to Portugal, to the address _____, within __ (months/days).
>
> [Signature]

PORTUGAL BACKGROUND CHECK AUTHORIZATION

DECLARAÇÃO DE AUTORIZAÇÃO

Eu,_____, filho(a) de
_____ e de_____, nascido(a) aos
_____, de nacionalidade _____, portador(a) do
passaporte n.o _____, requerente de visto de Residência/
Estada Temporária para efeitos de _____, autorizo, nos
termos da alínea d) do n.o1 do art. 12 do Decreto Regulamentar
2/2013, de 18 de Março, a consulta pelo Serviço de Estrangeiros e
Fronteiras do meu registo criminal português.

_____, aos ___ de _____ de 20__

AUTHORIZATION STATEMENT

I, [YOUR FULL NAME], NIF [NIF NUMBER], [SON/DAUGHTER] of
[FATHER'S NAME] and of [MOTHER'S NAME], of nationality
UNITED STATES OF AMERICA, bearer of passport at UNITED
STATES OF AMERICA, [PASSPORT NUMBER], valid until
[EXPIRATION DATE]; [MARITAL STATUS], with tax domicile in
[STATE], USA; applicant for a Residence/Temporary Stay visa for
the purpose of [RETIREMENT/OTHER], authorize, under the terms
of subparagraph d) of Nº. 1 of Art. 12 of Regulatory Decree 2/2013,
of 18 March, the consultation by the Foreigners and Borders
Service of my Portuguese criminal record.

[SIGNATURE]

[YOUR FULL NAME]

on [DAY] of [MONTH] of [YEAR]

Signature much match that on the identification document

SAMPLE PET ARRIVAL FORM

To [Airport] Veterinarian:
I will be arriving at [Airport] with [number] pets: [type]

As the owner/person authorized in writing by the owner to perform on his behalf the circulation without commercial purposes of the [animal], I hereby inform you that the animal that accompanies me will arrive to [arrival city] from [departure city] to [arrival] airport, Portugal in flight [number] on [date] with arrival time by [time].

The [animal] will travel: in the [cabin/luggage]. I am traveling from a low rabies risk country, the United States.

Please see the attached pages(s) that indicate(s) the microchip number and date of placing and the page(s) that indicate(s) the updated rabies vaccination.

Owner info:

Owners Full Name
Origination Address: Xxxx x street Xxxx, [ST] USA
Address in Portugal: xxxx xxxx, Portugal
US Phone: +1 xxx xxx xxxx PT Phone: +351 xxx xxx xxx
Email: Xxxxx@email.com
Dog: [animal description, color, age]

Signed   Date

The personal data collected in this form will be used exclusively to carry out all procedures necessary for the registration of the owners/authorized persons on behalf of the owners of non-commercial pets from countries outside the European Union at the time of notification of their arrival. I authorize the use of these data as explained above.

SOCIAL SECURITY DIRECT DEPOSIT

Form **SSA-1199**-PE (02-2021)
Discontinue Prior Editions
Social Security Administration

DIRECT DEPOSIT SIGN-UP FORM (PORTUGAL)

APPLICATION FOR PAYMENT OF UNITED STATES SOCIAL SECURITY
MONTHLY BENEFITS BY DIRECT DEPOSIT

- Complete Section 1 and "SIGN YOUR NAME"
- Ask your bank to complete Section 3
- Mail completed form back using address in Section 2

SECTION 1 (TO BE COMPLETED BY PAYEE)

Name and Complete Mailing Address:

SOCIAL SECURITY CLAIM NUMBER	B.I.C. (OPTIONAL)

Name of Person Entitled to the Benefits

Telephone Number:

THIS BOX IS FOR ALLOTMENT OF PAYMENT ONLY (if applicable)

Type	Amount

PAYEE CERTIFICATION	**JOINT ACCOUNT HOLDER'S CERTIFICATION** (optional)
I (beneficiary or representative payee) certify that I have read and understand the back of this form. In signing this form, I authorize the Social Security Administration to send this payment to the financial institution indicated in Section 3 and deposit it in the designated account. I understand that personal information in these payments is confidential, but I consent to disclosure of payment information compelled by law or necessary to protect against fraud or crime.	I certify that I have read and understand the back of this form, including the SPECIAL NOTICE TO JOINT ACCOUNT HOLDERS.

Your Signature	Date	Joint Account Holder's Signature	Date

Are you the Representative Payee? ☐ Yes ☐ No

Beneficiary Date of Birth

This account is:
☐ My own account   ☐ A joint account

SECTION 2 (MAILING ADDRESS)

GOVERNMENT AGENCY NAME:

SOCIAL SECURITY ADMINISTRATION

MAIL COMPLETED FORMS TO:
Federal Benefits Unit
U.S. Embassy
Avenida das Forcas Armadas
1600 Lisbon
Portugal

SECTION 3 (TO BE COMPLETED BY YOUR FINANCIAL INSTITUTION)
THIS ACCOUNT MUST BE IN EUROS

NAME OF BANK / NOMO DO BANCO	BANK PHONE NUMBER / NÚMERO DE TELEOFONE DEL BANCO

ADDRESS OF BANK
MORADA

PRINT NAME OF BANK OFFICIAL / NOME DO OFICIAL DE BANCO	SIGNATURE OF BANK OFFICIAL / ASSINATURA DORESPONSÁVEL PELA INFORMAÇÃO

Print the IBAN number in the blocks below. Fill all blocks.
IMPRIMA O NUMERO IBAN NOS BLOCOS ABAIXO.

Print the entire SWIFT/BIC code in the blocks below.
IMPRIMA TODO O CODIGO NOS BLOCOS ABAIXO

IMPORTANT INFORMATION - PLEASE READ CAREFULLY

The information you give on this form is confidential. We need the information to send your U.S. Social Security payments electronically to your Portugal bank account.

WHEN YOU WILL RECEIVE YOUR DIRECT DEPOSIT PAYMENTS

You will receive your payment through the Portugal banking system and will usually be in your bank account shortly after the regular payment date. With direct deposit, you will have immediate access to your money. This is the safest way of receiving your benefits.

INFORMATION ABOUT CURRENCY CONVERSION:

With direct deposit, your U.S. Social Security payment is automatically converted to Euros (if applicable) at the daily international exchange rate before being deposited to your account.

SPECIAL NOTICE TO JOINT ACCOUNT HOLDERS

If you have a joint account with a person who receives Social Security payments, and that person dies, you must immediately contact your bank and the Social Security Administration or the Federal Benefits Unit in your area. You must return to Social Security any payments deposited into a joint account after the death of a beneficiary.

IF YOUR ADDRESS CHANGES:

If your address changes, you **must** inform the Federal Benefits Unit or the Social Security Administration. Your payments may stop if the Social Security Administration needs to contact you and cannot find your location.

CHANGING BANKS OR BANK ACCOUNTS:

If you change your bank or your account, you must notify one of the following offices:

Federal Benefits Unit U.S. Embassy Avenida das Forcas Armadas 1600 Lisbon Portugal	Social Security Administration Office of Earnings and International Operations Division Of International Operations PO Box 17769 Baltimore, MD 21235-7769 USA

You may need to fill out a new Direct Deposit sign-up form.
Do not close your old account until payments have started coming to your new account.

Privacy Act Statement
Collection and Use of Personal Information

Section 205(a) of the Social Security Act, as amended, allows us to collect this information. Furnishing us this information is voluntary. However, failing to provide all or part of the information may prevent you from receiving benefit payments through foreign financial institutions.

We will use the information you provide to process benefit payments with your financial institution. We may also share your information for the following purposes, called routine uses:

- To the Department of State and its agents for administering the Act in foreign countries through facilities and services of that agency; and

- To third party contacts where necessary to establish or verify information provided by representative payees or payee applicants.

In addition, we may share this information in accordance with the Privacy Act and other Federal laws. For example, where authorized, we may use and disclose this information in computer matching programs, in which our records are compared with other records to establish or verify a person's eligibility for Federal benefit programs and for repayment of incorrect or delinquent debts under these programs.

A list of additional routine uses is available in our Privacy Act System of Records Notices (SORN) 60-0089, entitled Claims Folders Systems, as published in the Federal Register (FR) on April 1, 2003, at 68 FR 15784 and 60-0090, entitled Master Beneficiary Record, as published in the FR on January 11, 2006, at 71 FR 1826. Additional information and a full listing of all our SORNs are available on our website at https://www.ssa.gov/privacy.

Paperwork Reduction Act Statement

This information collection meets the requirements of 44 U.S.C. § 3507, as amended by section 2 of the Paperwork Reduction Act of 1995. You do not need to answer these questions unless we display a valid Office of Management and Budget control number. We estimate that it will take about 5 minutes to read the instructions, gather the facts, and answer the questions. **SEND OR BRING THE COMPLETED FORM TO YOUR LOCAL SOCIAL SECURITY OFFICE. You can find your local Social Security office through SSA's website at** www.socialsecurity.gov. **Offices are also listed under U. S. Government agencies in your telephone directory or you may call Social Security at 1-800-772-1213 (TTY 1-800-325-0778).** *You may send comments on our time estimate above to: SSA, 6401 Security Blvd, Baltimore, MD 21235-6401. **Send only comments relating to our time estimate to this address, not the completed form.***

PERSONAL HEALTH HISTORY

Name:	
Birthdate:	
Height:	
Weight:	
Marital Status:	
Blood Type:	
Emergency Contact: (primary, PT)	
Emergency Contact: (secondary, PT)	
Emergency Contact: (secondary, USA)	
ALLERGIES	

INDICATE ALL YOU NOW HAVE OR HAVE EVER HAD:	YES / WHEN?
Rheumatic fever or chorea?	
Jaundice, liver, kidney disease or hepatitis?	
A heart murmur or heart problem, angina, blood pressure, or heart attack?	

A reaction to a general or local anesthetic?	`
A joint replacement or other implant?	
Growth hormones before the mid 1980s?	
High cholesterol?	
High blood pressure?	
Cancer?	
Psoriasis?	
Pneumonia?	
Pulmonary embolism?	
Asthma?	
Emphysema?	
Stroke?	
Epilepsy (seizures)?	
Cataracts?	
Kidney disease?	
Kidney stones?	
Diabetes?	
DO YOU:	**NOTES:**
Have arthritis?	
Have a pacemaker?	

Suffer from hay fever, eczema or any other allergy?	
Suffer from bronchitis, asthma, or any other chest condition?	
Have fainting attacks, blackouts, or epilepsy?	
Bruise easily or persistently bleed following injury, tooth extraction, or surgery?	
Suffer from any infectious diseases (including HIV)?	
Smoke or vape?	
Drink alcohol? Amount?	
Exercise? Frequency?	

SURGERIES

TYPE	DATE	HOSPITAL	NOTES

SERIOUS ILLNESSES

NAME	START	END	HOSPITAL	NOTES

MEDICATIONS
(including non-prescription, supplements, etc.)

NAME	DOSAGE	FREQUENCY	DATE STARTED	PRESCRIBER

PREVENTIVE SCREENINGS

TYPE	FREQUENCY	DATE OF LAST TEST	RESULTS	LOCATION	NOTES

IMMUNIZATIONS

TYPE	FREQUENCY	DATE OF LAST TEST	LOCATION	NOTES

MY PROVIDERS

NAME	SPECIALTY	CONTACT DETAILS	LAST VISIT

CHRONIC CONDITIONS

TYPE	TREATMENTS/ MEDICATIONS	PROVIDER	NOTES

FAMILY HISTORY

RELATIONSHIP	AGE	AGE AT DEATH	CAUSE (IF DECEASED)
Father			
Mother			
Sibling			
Sibling			
Sibling			
Child			
Child			

CANCER HISTORY IN FAMILY

RELATIONSHIP TO PATIENT	MATERNAL	PATERNAL	CANCER TYPE/SITE	AGE AT DIAGNOSIS

Made in United States
Orlando, FL
04 August 2024